فتوح الغيب

Futuh Al Ghaib

The Revelations of the Unseen

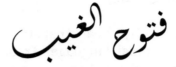

Futuh Al Ghaib

The Revelations of the Unseen

Muhyuddin Abdul Qadir Gilani

Translator

Aftab Ud Din Ahmad

2022 CE – 1443 H

Translation of the Qur'ān

It should be perfectly clear that the Qur'ān is only authentic in its original language, Arabic. Since perfect translation of the Qur'ān is impossible, we have used the translation of the meaning of the Qur'ān throughout the book, as the result is only a crude meaning of the Arabic text.

Qur'ānic verses appear in speech marks proceeded by a reference to the Surah and verse number. Sayings (*Hadith*) of Prophet Muhammad (saw) appear in inverted commas along with reference to the Hadith Book and its Reporter.

TO

THE LOVING MEMORY OF MY UNCLE
SAYYID IRSHAD ALI

*who was so patient with me in all my inquiries, who was
the only member of my family who was really happy to
see me take a sudden turn for religion, who was always
anxious for the dissemination of the real teachings of
Islam and who ended his life as a true Sufi*

THE HUMBLE WORK OF TRANSLATION
IS DEDICATED

PUBLISHER'S NOTE

All the references in brackets refer to the passages from The Holy Qur'an. Roman numerals indicate the number of the Suarh (Chapter) and Arabic numerals state the 'Ayat' (Sentence).

Contents

Introduction

Hazrat Syed Abdul Qadir Gilani—the Saint of Baghdad (mercy of Allah upon him)—does not stand in need of an introduction to the Muslim world. Among the books associated with his name, the *Futuh al-Ghaib* has acquired a fame that falls to the lot of very few works of this kind. Born in a province whose people are highly imaginative and mystical by nature, I felt quite early in my life drawn towards the personality of this Saint. The later rationalistic meanderings of my mind, however, disturbed the natural development of this admiration. It was, however, at the suggestion of a Bengali Muslim friend that I ultimately made up my mind to go through this particular book with a scrutiny that would enable me to present to the English-speaking world the precious gems that fell from the lips of this great mystic of the Middle East. The fruits of my first labour, however, were not so happy . . . .

The book is evidently mystical, though not too mystical for an average intelligent man with a little introspection. It seems that the world is too much taken up with questions of material existence to find any time for a study of this nature. And yet the social and political upheavals all the world over, making the question of life and existence so uncertain, have, I believe, created a proper psychological background for the study of such a book as this. I should not be taken to mean that I am suggesting or that Islam suggests an escapist attitude under such circumstances. Islam never tries to create the escapist mentality nor does the present book encourage such a frame of mind. We are, however, for a change in the mental out-look of man which will bring about an actual solution of the tangles confronting our species in this age. It is not difficult to see that the lack of a higher vision of life has resulted in an over-emphasis on comparatively less important aspects of our worldly existence, which in its turn has been the root cause of all our strifes. It is hoped that a perusal of books such as this will open the eyes of people to that higher vision and lessen the heat of ruinous competition in the field of material acquisition.

The Arabic text in my hand is the one which is to be found in an Urdu translation of the book entitled *Futuh al-Ghaib Mutarjam*, by Maulvi Sikandar Shah of Benares. As this translator assures us in his introduction, he took great pains in securing the complete and correct text of the original Arabic before he took up his work of Urdu translation, and yet the text which accompanies this translation is not free from mistakes some of which are extremely disappointing. One will understand what I mean if one examines carefully pages 46 to 49. In spite of this drawback, the text may be regarded as fairly dependable and helpful in that it provides vital points which are fairly accurate. As for the Urdu translation itself, though rather free here and there, it undoubtedly shows the deep learning of the translator as well as his acquaintance with matters connected with Islamic spiritual science, otherwise known as *tasawwuf*.

A few words about this science will, I hope, be of use to such of the readers as are not conversant with the traditions of Islam. The word "mysticism" which is generally used to indicate this aspect of Islam is a little misleading. The English word has an elusive atmosphere about it, whereas "tasawwuf" is a regular science with its set laws and a full scheme in detail. It is based on palpable experiences which can be reproduced, like in any other science, under set circumstances. Every pilgrim has to pass through the same stages in his spiritual journey and these stages are readily recognisable by their detailed descriptions given unanimously by all masters. The landmarks and pitfalls are described in equally exhaustive particulars. Just as in any other course of study, there are methods in it to test the progress of the disciple and his merit. As in any other branch of knowledge, there are geniuses in this branch of study who create a stir in the world, but even the humblest learner can at least aspire to develop a living sense of the presence of God in the midst of our struggle for material existence. He also develops a taste for this culture and an interest in those who follow this path and thereby acquires an increasing control over his passions and desires for things worldly. It can be readily understood that this paves the way for real social peace, the crying need of the times. As for the more gifted pilgrims, but for them God would be a mere hypothesis. It is these experiences that have made God a palpable fact of experience and have made think·ng humanity believe in the continuity of life after death. It is they who radiate a faith in life everlasting which in its turn takes away the sting from death and enables us, average men, to view life with a sense of ease. They attain to a perfect certainty about the existence of God by a speaking contact with Him and thereby act as the vicegerents of the Holy Prophet (may Allah's peace and bles\;ings be upon him). It is to these people that the Holy Prophet refe1s in his oft-quoted saying: "The learned among my followe1s are like the prophets of Israel" or in another saying: "The learned are the successors of the Prophets "

The law being complete in the shape of the Holy Qur'an, no Prophet is needed after the Holy Prophet (may Allah's peace and blessings be upon him) yet these spiritual luminaries must be there to testify to the existence of God, to the truth of the Qur'anic revelation, and to the continuity of the Holy Prophet's spiritual regime. Without these personalities belief in all these verities will be reduced into a mere makebelieve, devoid of any power to influence people's thought and action. This has exactly been the fate of all religions excepting Islam, which, though professed by a politically backward people at the moment, is yet rich in the tradition of these living experiences.

I, therefore, appeal to the scientific-minded people of other faiths to read these discourses carefully and ascertain for themselves if their approach is not a perfectly scientific one. And we should bear in mind that this is only one of many such works by people of this line. In fact, it is these works that have saved Islamic theology from appearing the dry thing which it is in every other religion. It is not here a speculative philosophy or a dogmatic theology, but an experimental science with its attractions as such. To describe briefly the general framework of this science, human consciousness is divided into three conditions rising upward in the scale of evolution:

1. *Nafs Ammara*, i.e. unruly animal self.
2. *Nafs Lawwama*, i e. struggling moral self.
3. *Nafs Mutmainna*, i.e. composed Allah-realised self.

In the first stage man is a pure animals, restless self-animal urges, impatient of restrictions and stranger to any pricking of conscience. By a systematic course of religious training, of which obedience to commands and prohibitions is the chief feature, he develops a sense of propriety and impropriety and repents after every falling into error. This is the *Lawwama* state. This stage begins with a faint dawning of the moral sense and ends in a complete surrender of the animal ego in man, which marks the third and the highest stage, viz. *Mutmainna*. The struggle between the lower and the higher selves having now ended, the pilgrim enters a condition of perfect peace, of purity, of rectitude, and of knowledge.

To indicate the experiences, starting from the threshold of this stage, further on, the Sufis have coined three more terms:

1. *Fana*. A complete subjugation of the animal self. At this stage man ceases to be disturbed by any urge of desire. The only urge left in him is prayerful surrender of his whole being.

2. *Baqa*. This means a restoration of the self in a new consciousness, this time not of the flesh but of the spirit. The urges of the self are no longer from the animal passions which drive a person to acts involving violation of others' rights and this leading to disturbance in the society, but from Allah-controlled spiritual region, the source of actions invariably beneficial to humanity and creation.

3. *Liqa*. This is the stage wherein man's spiritual knowledge rises to such a high pitch that the rewards for his faith, sincerity and devotion no longer remain a matter of belief but a palpable certainty and an experience, as if he has then already and his faith in Allah reaches a point wherein it seems to him that he is seeing Him face to face. Such a man becomes free from all fears about the future and from all sorrows about the present and past. In such a condition a man is free from all hesitation and obscurity of judgment and doubts and misgivings. In this condition the devotee is coloured by the attributes of Allah in the manner of a piece of iron, assuming the colour of fire if it is kept long enough in it. And in moments of commotion such a man's feelings partake of Divine-powers, so much so that this pleasure brings in the pleasure and blessing of Allah and his anger brings the wrath and curse of Allah, and events seem-

ingly contrary to the laws of nature come into being through his attention. Receiving powers from Allah he possesses a power of creation. He creates events and even determines the course of history.

It should be borne in mind that after a pilgrim has entered the state of *Fana,* which in the language of the Qur'an is called "Istiqama," the next two stages of *Baqa* and *Liqa* follow as a matter of course. The reason is that when a person becomes completely void of attachment to creation and desires and personal will, he automatically enters the state of *Baqa.* And so long as a man is not confirmed in the state of self-annihilation his surrender to Allah does not become a spontaneous affair, he cannot be said to be in the state of *Baqa,* which requires that all acts of devotion and surrender should become natural acts, not needing any effort. When such a state is attained, the man feels that all that belongs to him is really Allah's. And while other people of the world relish the satisfaction of their personal desires, such a person enjoys the worship of Allah and His remembrance.[1]

Thus, when the pligrim is confirmed in this state of *Baqa* and it becomes the warp and woof of his very being, a light appears to descend from heaven and mist of uncertainty is altogether lifted from his heart, which is filled now with a sweet feeling of love, never experienced before, like the one which one experiences at the time of reunion with a loving friend after a long separation. This is accompanied by a highly pleasing shower of Divine communications every now and then which may be said to be attended by a heavenly sweet smell and a coolness like that of spring breeze. At this stage the devotee feels pleasure in sacrificing his everything for the sake of Allah, even his honour and life. His heart gets so filled with Light Divine that it seems if he is experiencing the rays of the midday sun within his bosom and as if Allah Himself has descended on his heart with all His glory. And these are the signs of the state of *Liqa.*

It is also to be remembered that, while attainment of *Fana* is the result of human efforts, the two higher stages *Baqa* and

1. *Vide Aina-i-Kamalat-i-Islam.*

Liqa are the gifts of Allah proceeding from His grace. The pilgrim's spiritual struggles take him up to the stage of *Fana* only. After this, Divine grace takes him by the hand and carries him to the higher regions. So the rigours of journey are felt only up to the stage of *Fana*.

It seems also necessary to explain another set of ideas and corresponding terms in Sufism. It is in relation to the order of saints. According to the Sufis, there is a hierarchy of Saints (*or awliya*) at all times in the world, through whom Allah manifests His mercy in the world of humanity. In the absence of the Prophet they are the vicegerents of Allah on earth on his behalf. They are of three different grades—*Badal* (*pl.—Abdal*). *Ghauth*, and *Qutub*. *Badal*—literally "substitute"—is so called because if any one of these saints happens to pass away, Allah immediately substitutes him by another (*Sihah*). They are righteous persons of whom the world is never destitute (Ibn Durayd, *Sihah Muhkam, Qamus*). But more authoritative view is that they are given this name because of their ever-changing spiritual condition. They are in a flux and are not allowed to remain in one state. Being still on their way to Allah-realisation they are not allowed to settle down at any intermediate point. As to their exact number and their postings, opinions are divided. They seem to be the lowest in rank among the spiritual successors of the Prophet.

Ghauth and Qutub. According to the best authorities, "they are a hierarchy of the saints of a particular generation, and are supposed to be pre-eminently endowed with sanctity and with miracle-working faculties. It anybody is *Qutub* or a *Ghauth*, he is recognised as such only by his agents, *Badals*, unless, of course, he himself reveals his position to a particular man. The literal meaning of *Qutub* is "axis," or "pivot," the point upon which a thing turns, "the chief upon whom the state of affairs turns." So a *Qutub* is he whose attention and prayers decide the course of events in a particular society of people. He may be regarded as a kind of spiritual agent in a particular community. The literal meaning of *Ghauth* is "aid," "succour" in the midst of difficulties. So a *Ghauth* is a kind of intercessor who intercedes at a moment when the sins of a nation or humanity are at the point of being punished. These seem to be particularly tender-hearted like the Holy Prophet Muhammad (may peace and blessings of Allah be upon him) himself, whose hearts melt at the woes and sufferings of humanity and who are, therefore, a means to avert Divine punishment. With the acceptability of their prayers assured, their prayers become a plea for Divine forgiveness and mercy. So *Badal* or *Abdal* may be regarded as spiritual magistrates. Above them are the *Qutubs* and in the highest rank are the *Ghauth*.

Together they constitute the make-weight of spiritual humanity at the particular moment, acting on behalf and under the stamp of the Holy Prophet—peace and blessings of Allah be upon him. But unlike the *Mujaddids* who are not only authorised but even commanded to announce their existence and authority, not to speak of the *Abdal*, neither the *Qutub*, nor even the *Ghauth* are authorised to proclaim their existence and position. They act in silence, serve humanity by their precepts and examples and pray incessantly for the general forgiveness of human sins.

Some people have contended that the idea that such people exist and that they are a kind of intercessors for humanity is not Islamic. A perusal of verses 20-27 of *Sura* Yasin (The Holy Qur'an) will show that even in a nation doomed to destruction for its inequities, there live persons who testify to the truth of a Prophet appearing among them by their power of readily recognising the will of Allah. The event is begun with the following words :

"And from the remote part of the country there came a man running, he said 'O my people ! follow the meassenger." (xxxvi-20).

Now, who was this man ? I suggest it was either a *Ghauth* or a *Qutub* .

As for the idea that punishment for the sin of a nation is averted by the presence of an eminent man of spirituality, this can be deduced from the story of Prophet Lot as given in *Sura* Hud (The Holy Qur'an). This narration shows that the punishment even of a doomed nation is deferred out of a deference to a spiritual personality living in its midst. Even the punishment of the Quraish was deferred till the migration of the Holy Prophet (may Allah's peace and blessings be upon him) from Mecca. The Holy Qur'an lays down this principle in so many words : "Nor is Allah going to chastise them while you are among them" (viii-33). So the idea of the Sufis can be traced to principles laid down in the Holy Qur'an itself apart from its verification by invariable experiences of saints throughout our history.

The well-known hadith (Code of Islamic Conduct as preached and practised by Prophet Muhammad, may Allah's peace and blessings be upon him) ascribing to Allah the words :

"One who is hostile to My *Wali* receives an announcement of war from Me".

presents only the counterpart of this idea. Because if hostility to a *Wali* excites the wrath of Allah, his attention and prayers must be able to draw the mercy of Allah. Of source, the *Wali* spoken of here is of the higher type, which forms the subject of our discussion.

A few words would also seem necessary in explanation of another set of terms used in the pages that follow. It is again a trio—*Siddiq, Shahid* and *Salih*. But unlike the previous set these terms are no creation of the Sufis but are Qur'anic in origin. It is the Holy Qur'an which divides those favoured by Allah into four groups—Prophets, *Siddiqs, Shahids* and *Salihs* (iv-69). The circle of the first group has been closed after the appearance of the Holy Prophet Muhammad (may Allah's peace and blessings be upon him), because Divine law has reached its completion in the Holy Qur'an. But the other three groups are to continue extending their circles till the end of human history.

Siddiqs are next to the Prophets in rank. The root word is *Sidq* meaning "truth" and the particular word indicates an intensified form of this quality. Thus *Siddiq* may be said to be an embodiment of truth. Strict truthfullness in speech is the minimum requirement. Conformity of speech with action and a deep inalienable love for truth in all its forms are its higher demands. Such a person recognises truth in all its manifestations. He hates the very semblance of falsehood and.

loves truth in all its manifold phases. Hazrat Abu Bakr Siddiq (may Allah be pleased with him) was a type of this. This is why his epithet "Siddiq". He recognised the prophethood of the Holy Prophet (may Allah's peace and blessings be upon him) without asking either for argument or for miracles. Then his constant companionship of the Holy Prophet (may Allah's peace and blessings be upon him) at all kinds of risks, particularly at that most critical moment of his life when he migrated from Mecca to Medina to be away from his enemies who were thirsting for his blood, shows that his attachment to truth was not confined to his thought and speech but it went deeper and sank in his very being. It was this devotion to truth that gave him that unshakable faith which enabled him to withstand the utter confusion that followed the Holy Prophet's (may Allah's peace and blessings be upon him) demise and threatened the budding spiritual commonwealth with disruption.

Next in grade comes the *Shahid*. The root word is *Shahida*, i.e. he witnessed or experienced. A *Shahid* reaches a state of spiritual journey wherein he may be said to be witnessing the glory and power of Allah. He feels as if he is in His very presence. The spiritual values of things and people which are hypothetical and are matters of belief to an ordinary pilgrim and hence have to be maintained with an effort are to the *Shahid* manifest truths, for which he would pay any price. Acts of virtue proceed from him spontaneously as out of natural desires. Hence he feels pleasure at sacrificing everything that he has at the altar of truth. One need not actually be killed to prove oneself a *Shahid*, but one must be fully prepared to die a martyr's death at all moments of one's life.

The last in the grade comes the *Salih*. The root word is *Salaha* (he became sound or healthy). It is the barest requirement of spiritual health that a man should relish devotional practices. He should enjoy religious acts. For such a relish he should first be cleansed of all impure elements in his spiritual being—such as insincerity, greed, jealousy, show and ostentation pride and arrogance, cruelty, etc. He must be, so to speak a living embodiment of piety and moral caution, the minimum qualification for a Godly man.

A word more to the non-Muslim readers of this book. It has been suggested by outsiders that Sufism is a borrowed plume and not of the soul of Islam. This is based on crass ignorance. All the affairs that led to the formation of the Islamic society and civilisation were based on the verbal revelation coming to the Holy Prophet (may Allah's peace and blessings be upon him) in moments of spiritual trance and minor revelation coming to his companions every now and then are indisputable facts of history. Exclusive devotional practices of a whole band of disciples called *As-hab-e-Suffa* are also among the outstanding facts of the Prophet's time. To say in face of this that Islam was a dogmatic and ritualistic faith in its origin and that *tasawwuf* was a later growth is to deny a broad daylight fact of history. The fact is that *tasawwuf* is the soul of Islam and political Islam its physical manifestation. Of course, much of what passes for Sufism is not *tasawwuf*. Ideas and practices foreign to Islam and even antagonistic to it have undoubtedly entered the body politic even of this living faith, particularly for the last few centuries, because of the general decadence in the Islamic socio-intellectual order. But disease does not prove the non-existence of health altogether nor decay the non-existence of body. In spite of corrupting influences from outside and their effects on our spiritual system, *tasawwuf* in its pristine purity has throughout existed in the Islamic society. It needs eyes, however, to see it. Eyes that can see nothing but howling and dancing *darwishes* as samples of Islamic mysticism, must undergo a major spiritual operation to be fit to discover *tasawwuf* in Islam.

In conclusion, I pray in all humility to the All-Merciful Allah that He may make me and the readers inspired by the words such as those that follow to follow the path of these luminaries of spiritual humanity to the best of out efforts. Ameen.

The Qur'anic verses in English have been taken from the work of Muhammad Ali, the pioneer translator of the Holy Book into English. May Allah bless him for this sacred work!

AFTAB-UD-DIN-AHMAD

A Life–Sketch of Ghauth al–Azam Mohy-ud-Din Sayyid Abdul Qadir Gilani

PARENTAGE

Sayyid Abu Muhammad Abdul Qadir was born in Naif in the District of Gilani in Persia in the month of Ramadan in the year 470 A.H. corresponding to 1077 of the Christian era or thereabout. His father's name was Abu Salih, a God-fearing man and a direct descendant of Hazrat Imam Hasan, the eldest son of Hazrat Ali, Karrammallahu Wajhu the Holy Prophet's first cousin, and of Bibi Fatima (may Allah's blessings be upon her) his beloved daughter. His mother was the daughter of a saintly person — Abdullah Sawmai who was a direct descendant of Imam Husain, the younger son of Hazrat Ali and Bibi Fatima. Thus Sayyid Abdul Qadir was both Hasani and Husaini (may peace and blessings of Allah be upon them all).

EARLY LIFE

From his early childhood he was quiet and sober, given to contemplation and used to what, for want of a better expression, is called 'mystic experiences' in English. When he was about eighteen years old his thirst for knowledge and eagerness for the company of holy men took him to the distant city of Baghdad, at that time the centre of learning of all kinds. Later in life he was given the title of 'Ghauth-al-Azam Dastgir', i.e. the greatest of all saints called *Ghauth*. In the Sufi terminology a *Ghauth* is next to a *Nabi* in spiritual rank and in the dispensation of Divine mercy and favour to mankind. A great authority of

1

our times, however, has ranked him with the *Siddiqun*, as the Qur'an would call such people. And he bases his view on an incident that took place in the course of the first journey of the Shaikh to Baghdad. It is related that as he was about to leave home on this momentous journey his widowed mother sewed eighty gold coins inside his coat just below his armpits as a provision against hard times. This money was his share of the patrimony. As he was taking leave of his mother, a saintly mother of a saintly son, her parting advice was that he should not speak an untruth at any cost whatsoever. The son promised to bear this advice always in mind. The caravan with which he travelled had gone only as far as Hamadan when it encountered a gang of robbers. In the course of their loot the robbers did not take much notice of him because he looked quite simple and poor. One of them, however, casually asked him if he had any money on him. The young Abdul Qadir, remembering his promise to his mother, unhesitatingly replied, "Yes, I have eighty gold pieces sewn into my garment by my mother". The robbers were astonished to hear him make this statement. They could not imagine a man could be so truthful as that. They took him to their leader, who put the same question to him and his reply was the same as before. The leader then ordered that the particular part of his coat be opened and, as it was opened, the eighty gold coins were found as stated. The robber chief's astonishment knew no bounds. He inquired of the young traveller the basis of this surprising veracity. The Shaikh related all that had taken place between himself and his mother at the time of parting and added that if he had told a lie on the very first stage of his journey undertaken for the sake of religious knowledge, he had obviously no chance of acquiring any real knowledge of religion at subsequent stages of his career. On hearing this the leader of the gang burst into tears, fell down at his feet and repented for all past sins. It is reported that he was his first disciple. Our authority is of opinion that this incident showed the *Siddiq* in the making. Had his very nature not been truthful in origin, such a courageous and unwavering stand for truth, in the face of such heavy odds, would not have been possible for him.

A STUDENT IN BAGHDAD

Truthful and charitable to the extreme, he had to endure great hardships during the period of his study at Baghdad. By dint of his natural talents and devotion he became very soon the master of all the different subjects that could be learnt by a scholar in those days. He proved to be the greatest jurist of his time. But his deeper spiritual yearnings were restless to manifest themselves. Even in his adolescence when he was engaged in his studies he was fond of *mujahida* or the struggle to conquer the self to rise above his animal self. He often resorted to fasting and would not ask for food from anyone even if he had to go without any meal for days together. He used to find out the spiritually-minded in Baghdad and cultivate intimacy with them. It was in the course of this search that he came across Hazrat Hammad, a vendor of syrups but a great saint of his time. Gradually this saint became a sort of a spiritual tutor to our hero. Hazrat Hammad, however, was a very dry and harsh kind of person and his treatment to our budding Sufi was extremely severe. But our would-be *Ghauth* bore all this as a kind of corrective for his own spiritual defects.

SPIRITUAL EXERCISES

After he finished his studies he became more severe on his own self. He began to deny himself all the needs and comforts of life excepting the barest minimum that would sustain life. The time and energy he would thus save he would employ in prolonged prayers and in the reading of the Holy Qur'an. So engrossed did he become in his prayers that he could be seen saying his morning prayers with the ablution performed for the prayers of the previous night. It is reported that very often he was seen finishing the recitation of the whole Qur'an in a single night. During this period he avoided all contacts with people and would not meet or talk to any one. If he went out he would roam about in the deserts. Eventually he left Baghdad and came to stay at Shustar, a place twelve days' journey from Baghdad. For eleven years he thus shut himself out from the world. The end of this period marked the end of his training as

well. He received the illumination, as it is called. His animal
self had by now vacated his soul in favour of his higher being.
He was now established in Allah-consciousness.

TEMPTED BY THE DEVIL

A spiritual event took place on the eve of this new role
which is narrated in the form of a story. Similar stories are
related of practically all religious figures known to history. It is
a story of temptation. It appears that all such stories express a
natural event of life in the language of allegory. We read, for
example, of the temptation of Prophet Jesus—how the devil took
him to the hill-top and from there showed him the kingdoms of
the world and asked Jesus to worship him if he wanted to be
the master of those kingdoms. We know the memorable reply
of Jesus worthy of his position as a spiritual leader of men. For
all we know it might be just an event of inner struggle of the
master at a delicate point of his life.* An incident of this nature
also took place in the life of the most historical of all religious
personalities—I mean the Holy Prophet Muhammad (may
Allah's peace and blessings be upon him). When he persisted in
his preachings against the idolatrous practices of his country-
men, his opponents, the leaders of the Quraish, tempted him with
their offers of beauty, wealth and power. And no Muslim can
ever forget his memorable reply on this occasion—"I want neither pelf nor power. I have been commissioned by Allah as a
warner unto mankind, deliver His message to you. Should you
accept it you shall have felicity in this life as well as in the life
to come. Should you reject the word of Allah, surely Allah will
decide between you and me".

It was not a vision in this case but a solid fact of earthly
existence.

Quite in keeping with this tradition a story is narrated about
Shaikh Abdul Qadir Gilani which has two versions. One version
is that one day the Devil or Satan appeared before him, introdu-
ced himself as Gabriel and said that he had brought from Allah
the Burraq (i.e. the lightning conveyance on which the Holy

* St. Matthew, 4 : 8-11.

Prophet rode to the heavens on the night of his spiritual ascen-
sion called *Mi'raj* as he had been invited by Him to be in His
August Presence in the highest heaven. To this the Shaikh promp-
tly replied that the speaker of these words before him could be
no other than the Devil because neither Gabriel nor the Burraq
could come to the world for any person other than the Holy
Prophet Muhammad (may Allah's peace and blessings be upon
him). Satan, however, had still another missile to throw. He
said, "Well, Abdul Qadir, you have saved yourself by dint of
your knowledge." "Be off Satan," the Saint retorted, "do not
tempt me any further; it is not through my knowledge but
through the grace of Allah that I have escaped from your trap."

The other version of the story is that once the Shaikh was
in the wilderness and was without food and drink for a long
time. A cloud appeared overhead and showered rain. The
Shaikh quenched his thirst with it. Presently a luminous figure
appeared on the horizon and said, "I am your Allah, I now
make all unlawful things lawful for you." At this the Shaikh
recited the formula, "I seek the protection of Allah from Satan
the accursed." At this the figure changed into a cloud and it was
heard saying, "By your knowledge and by the grace of Allah
you have been saved from my deception." Then the Satan asked
the Shaikh how he could recognise him so quickly. The
Shaikh replied that his announcement making unlawful things
lawful betrayed him, because such an announcement could not
have been from Allah.

This story has a similarity with the vision of Peter.* But
whereas this great disciple of Jesus, falling a prey to the Devil's
deception, abrogated the law about prohibited food, throwing
into the winds the clear words of the Scripture and lifelong
practice of the master, this brave son of the Arab Prophet tore
into shreds the Devil's snare with the ease of an adept soldier.

As for the two versions of the story under discussion I am
inclined to think that both of them may be correct, presenting
two different incidents in an allegorical language. One incident
might relate to his struggle with pride of knowledge. The other

* The Acts, 10.

may refer to his struggle with economic difficulties which side-
track a man in his spiritual journey. Consciousness of power
and anxiety for comforts are the last weaknesses to leave the
mind of a spiritual pilgrim. And it is only after one has overcome these two eternal enemies of spirituality that one becomes
qualified to be a genuine leader of men.

A TEACHER OF PEOPLE

Now that the Shaikh had passed these tests if he spoke anything or admonished anyone it was not from the intellectual
plane any longer, but from the spiritual plane—the plane of
self-realisation. At this stage when he received the inner commandment, as the Shaikh himself would like to call it, to
preach, Islamic faith had grown weak. The Muslims were either
given to sensual pleasures or were satisfied with the rites and
rituals of religion. The spirit of religion was to be found no-
where in its native brilliance. About this time he had a signi-
ficant vision having a bearing on the question. It was on a
Friday in the year 511 A.H. He saw in the vision as if he were
walking along a street in Baghdad, where a sick and emaciated
man lying on the roadside greeted him with the Islamic salutation. When the Shaikh answered the salutation, the man asked
him to help him to sit up. On the Saint's giving him the help
asked for, the man sat up and began to grow miraculously big
in stature. Seeing the Saint frightened at the phenomenon, the
stranger allayed his fear saying "I am the religion of your
grandfather, I became diseased and miserable, but Allah has
revived me throguh your help." This happened on the eve of
his public appearance in the mosque and as such foreshadowed
the future career of the Saint. Later in life the enlightened
public conferred on him the title of *Mohy-ud-Din or* "the reviver
of the faith," a title which has since then been regarded as a
part of his illustrious name. But although he emerged from his
solitude, he would not take to public preaching even now. For
another eleven years he lived in a corner of the city and carried
on with his devotional practices acquiring more and more inner
illumination.

It was at the end of this period, i.e. A.H. 522, that he began to impart his knowledge to others. In this year he was given a *madrasa* to teach students. By now he was inwardly prepared for the task and had besides an inner commandment, as he calls it, for this new life. In the beginning, as was to be expected, he had a few students, but very soon his fame for learning, piety, inner illumination, veracity, and his strict adherence to the Shari'a spread far and wide and people from all over the world began to flock round him to reap the benefits of his lectures and sermons which covered all the aspects of life. Gradually the *madrasa* building proved too small for the ever-swelling number of students and pupils and the adjacent houses had to be acquired in 528 A.H. to enlarge the capacity of the building. Even this was not deemed sufficient for the demands of the eager public, to accommodate whom every Wednesday morning he would appear in the small Idgah and address the assembly from a platform raised for the purpose. When even this proved insufficient, he began to preach from the bigger Idgah situated outside the city, where subsequently a sort of sanctuary was built for him and this came to be known as *Musafirkhana.*

He used to deliver sermons thrice a week—at the Idgah on Friday mornings, at the *madrasa* on Tuesday nights, and at the *Musafirkhana* (Guest house) on Wednesday mornings. Different kinds of people came to him to learn different things. There were *Sufis* as well as *Faqihs* (i.e. students of jurisprudence), men of wealth as well as men of letters. Even non-Muslims attended these sermons and many of them embraced Islam at his hands. The Muslim sinners would suddenly change their course of life if they happened to listen to his discourses—such was the spiritual force at the back of his sermons. Indeed, the spiritual awe of his personality was so great that he was feared by the greatest men of the realm. The fact is that these spiritual personalities do not take to any occupation of their own choice. They surrender their whole being to their Creator and would not move in any matter unless they are directly handled by Allah and made to move in a particular affair. Public preaching is, therefore, no act of their own, and as such is not backed by any human preparation. Their preparation is done by Allah Himself and the whole inspiration for public preaching comes from Him direct. So when they speak they are prompted by the holy spirit of Allah. Hence the miraculous and revolutionary power of such utterances.

DOMESTIC LIFE

His public appearance, it is interesting to note, synchronises with his married life. Upto A.H. 521, i.e. the fifty-first year of his age, he never thought of marriage. He even regarded it as a sort of i npediment in the path of spiritual efforts. But as he came to establish contact with the people, in obedience to the commandment of the Holy Prophet (may Allah's peace and blessings be upon him) and in deference to his example he married four wives, all of whom were models of virtue and devoted to him. He had forty-nine children—twenty-seven sons and the rest daughters.

Four of his sons became noted for their erudition and learning.

(1) Shaikh Abdul Wahhab, the eldest born, was a great scholar and was given charge of the *madrasa* of his father in 543 A.H. After the Saint's expiry he also used to deliver sermons and give his opinions on questions of Islamic Shari'a. He also held an office under the State and was very popular.

(2) Shaikh Isa. He was a teacher of Hadith and a great jurist. He was also known to compose poems. He was a good preacher and also wrote books on Sufism. He settled down and finally died in Egypt.

(3) Shaikh Abdur Razzaq. He was a scholar and even a hafiz of Hadith. Like his father he had a reputation for truth-fulness. He possessed to some extent the spiritual trend of his father and became like him a very popular personality in Baghdad.

(4) Shaikh Musa was also a scholar of renown. He migrated to Damascus where he eventually died.

It was Shaikh Isa through whom the seventy eight discourses of the Saint have been handed down to us. His name is accordingly mentioned at the very beginning of this book. Abdul Wahhat is the source of the last two discourses that present an account of the Saint in the last moments of his worldly existence.

Shaikh Musa is mentioned towards the end of the book in the 79th and 80th discourses.

In the last two discourses a mention is made of two of the sons who were by the bedside of the Saint in his last moments — Abdul Razaq referred to above and Abdul Aziz.

USUAL OCCUPATIONS

As we have already seen, the Saint used to deliver three public sermons in a week. Besides these sermons every day in the morning and afternoon he used to give lessons on *Tafsir* or the commentary on the Qur'an, the Hadith, or the Traditions of the Prophet and principles of Islamic law and other allied subjects. After midday prayers he was seen issuing *fatwas* or verdicts on legal questions presented to him from all parts of the world. Every evening before the *Maghrib* prayers he would distribute food amongst the poor. After the evening prayers it was his habit to take his meals because usually he fasted during the day all throughout the year. But before every such meal it was his practice to have it proclaimed that anybody who needed food and was present in the neighbourhood could come and join him in his meals. After *Isha* prayers after the manner of all saintly persons he would retire to his chamber and spend the greater part of the night in the worship of Allah — a practice recommended by the Holy Qur'an for all who would claim to be in close spiritual relationship with the Holy Prophet (may Allah's peace and blessings be upon him). So like a true follower of the Prophet (may Allah's peace and blessings be upon him), he used to serve humanity all the hours of the day and serve his Creator during the greater part of the night.

DEATH

He breathed his last in 561 A.H. (1166 C.E.), at the age of ninety-one. The day was the 11th of Rabiussani. This date is commemorated by his admirers up to this day and is known as *Giarwin Sharif* in the Indo-Pakistan sub-continent.

HERITAGE

After the Saint's demise his sons and disciples continued his way of spiritual practices for the cultivation of real Islamic spirituality and dissemination of correct Islamic teachings among the people of the world. This was named after him as the *Qa'adariyyah* Order which is noted for its adherence to the principles of the Shari'a up to this day. In its own time it did great service to the general cause of Islam in the world and its contribution to the Islamic spiritual science has been enormous. Among the recorded teachings and exhortations of the Saint three are extant and enjoy worldwide reputation. The foremost of these is *Futuh al-Ghaib*, of which a translation is presented in the following pages.

Next in importance comes *Fath al-Rabbani* —a collection of sixty-eight sermons delivered in the years 545-6 A.H.

The third one is a *Qasida* or a poem that explains the role and rank of the Saint in an ecstatic language. It is called 'Qasidat al-Ghawthiyya'.

Like all other religious orders the *Qa'adariyyah* Order of our day seems more interested in this last mentioned treatise than in the other works that contain exhortations for self-improvement and convey a message from the world unseen.

But whatever the lapses of his latter-day admirers, the Saint's influence on Islamic history has been enormous and his personality shines out as a sparkling jewel of Islamic spirituality today as at all previous epochs of history.

Preliminary

The glory of the learned, the light of Iraq and Egypt, the spokesman of theologians, the interpreter of men of spiritual knowledge, the unique leader, the honour of religion, Shaikh Isa, Abu Abdul Rahman, mercy of Allah upon him and upon his progeny, said that:

My father the peerless chief, the most learned and possessed of very high and perfect spiritual knowledge, the leader of the leaders, the leader of nations, the chief of chiefs, the succour of men and the Jinn, the reviver of religion Abu Muhammad Abdul Qadir, son of Abu Salih, son of Abdullah, son of Yahya, the great ascetic, inhabitant of Jilan, may Allah sanctify his soul and illuminate his tomb said:

Praise be unto Allah—the Lord of the worlds, first and last, outwardly and inwardly, as many time as the number of His creations and equal to the measure of His words and to the weight of His throne and to the extent of His own pleasure and to the number of all things single and in pairs and of things wet and dry and of all that our Lord has created and spread for ever and—in all its purity and blessedness—praise to Him Who has created then made complete and Who has made things according to their measure and then guided (them to their goal), to Him Who causes death and gives life, Who makes one laugh and weep, Who makes one near and still closer, Who shows mercy and abases, Who gives food and drink, Who gives one good and bad luck, Who withholds gifts and then bestows them, by Whose command the seven strong heavens stand and the mountains are fixed like pegs and the spread-out earth is stayed and in Whose mercy no one can be disappointed and from Whose planning and enforcement of order and dignity and command, no one can escape and to Whose service no one can

11

be averse and of Whose blessings no one can be devoid; so He
is praised because He has been affectionate and He is given
thanks because He affords safety.

Then blessings on His Prophet Muhammad (may Allah's
peace and blessings be upon him) the chosen—anyone who
follows what he has brought receives guidance and whoever
turns away from him misguided and perishes—the truthful
Prophet of recognised truthfulness, abstainer from the world,
seeker of and inclined to the Friend on high, one who has been
chosen from among all His creatures and selected from the
whole of His creation, one with whose advent the truth has
come and with whose appearance falsehood has disappeared
and with whose light the earth is illuminated.

Let us once more invoke blessings on him—blessings abun-
dant and pure and blessed, as also on the pure among his
offspring, companions and his followers, together with His
favours—such of them as are best to their Lord in respect to
action and most right in respect of their words and most correct
in following His path. Next our entreaties and prayers and
recourse are to Him our Lord and Creator Who gives us food
and drink and confers benefit on us and protects us and keeps
us safe and gives us life and drives and keeps away from us all
that injures and gives us trouble and all this just out of His
mercy any compassion and as an act of favour and because of
His will to give us standing protection in all words and deeds,
in secret and in open and in our expressions and in our reti-
cence and in our straitened circumstances and in ease and comfort. Surely He is the absolute doer of whatever He likes and
orders whatever He wills, and knows whatever is hidden, and
is informed of all affairs and conditions both of sins and errors
as well as acts of obedience and states of nearness to Allah and
hears all noises and accepts all prayers from whomsoever He
likes and wills, without any contention and hesitation.

Now verily the favours of Allah are on His servants in
abundance and ceaselessly in all hours of night and day and at
all times and moments and in all conditions as Allah the Exalted has said: "And if you enumerate the favours of Allah you
will not be able to count them" (xiv-34). Elsewhere He the
Exalted says again: "And whatever of blessings is with you
it

is from Allah" (xvi-53). So I have neither the power nor the
heart nor yet the tongue with which I can count and enumerate
these blessings. Nor can numbers comprehend them, nor yet
can human thoughts and minds grasp them, nor yet can hearts
count them, nor yet can tongues describe them. So among the
blessings which He has enabled the tongue to describe and
power of speech to express and the fingers to record and the
power of description to describe are these few words that have
been revealed to me from the inspirations from the unseen
world and these alighted in my heart and filled up its space and
the return of normal state brought them out on the surface.
And then the favour and mercy of Allah the Lord of people
helped me to express words in a right form of speech to serve
as guidance for the seekers of truth.

The Qa'adariyyah Order is the main system of elevation on
the spiritual place. The Chishtia Order is the main offshoot
and all the other Orders are the branches varying on the
personal experiences of the leaders of the Orders.

Books like 'Futuh-al-Ghaib' and 'Fath-al-Rabbani' are in
the courses of study of the wayfarer on the path of attainment
the closeness of Allah, His Raza (willingness). The Murshid
(the spiritual guide or leader) strives to inculcate Islamic
discipline into the heart of the Mureed (a disciple who resolves
to purify his heart of all the things and thoughts worldly,
thereby to attain spiritual elevation), and the method so adopted or followed, comes to us, the readers, in the form of such
books. While we, the ordinary readers, read these books to
increase our knowledge, the Mureed goes through the experience
physically, mentally and spiritually till the attainment of
certainty. Living in the company of the Murshid, teaches a
Mureed more than what he can absorb through reading such
books. The Murshid invariably practices what he preaches and
becomes a living model amongst his Mureeds. No conversion
of hearts has ever taken place merely by reading books, com-
mentaries or explanations.

'Qasidat-al-Ghawthiyya' enjoys a unique place in the
spiritual journey. This poem is rich with spiritual vigour and
as such it has to be learnt by heart, and the Mureed has to·

include it in his Wazaif/Aurad (certain key words or sentences
as prescribed by the Murshid for the Mureed to be repeated
daily for a set number of times after his prayers). The Murshid
is a Perfect Master in the spiritual field and he is well aware of
the spiritual condition of his Mureed. Just as a physician knows
his patient and prescribes necessary medicines for eradication of
his physical ailments, so also the Murshid looks after the
welfare of his Mureed.

Futuh al–Ghaib

OR

The Revelations of the Unseen

In the name of Allah, the Beneficent, the Merciful

THE FIRST DISCOURSE

Three things are indispensable for a believer in all conditions
of life : he should keep the commandments of Allah; he should
abstain from the forbidden things; and he should be pleased
with the decree of Providence. Thus the least that is expected
of a believer is that he should not be without these three things.
So it is meant that he should make up his mind for this and
talk to himself about this and keep his organs engaged in this.

THE SECOND DISCOURSE

Follow faithfully in the footsteps of the Holy Prophet (may
Allah's peace and blessings be upon him) and do not create
innovation and remain obedient to Allah and His Prophet
(may Allah's peace and blessings be upon him) and do not
transgress; and uphold the Unity of Allah and do not ascribe
any partner to Him; and conceive Him in His Holiness and do
not ascribe any evil to Him; and maintain His truth and do
not give way to doubt; and remain patient and do not show
impatience; and remain firm and do not run away; and apply
to him for your needs but do not feel annoyed but wait; and be
united in obedience and do not be disunited; love one another
and do not bear spite towards one another; and keep free from

15

vices and do not be contaminated or defied by them; and beautify yourselves with obedience to your Lord; and do not remain away from the doors of your Master; and do not refrain from being attentive to Him; and do not delay your repentance and return to Him; and do not feel weary of making excuses to your Creator at any time during day and night; (if you do so) may be mercy will be shown to you and you will have good luck and be kept away from hell-fire and given a happy life in paradise and be united with Allah and enjoy the blessings of Allah together with the company of virgins in the Abode of Peace, and in that state abide for ever; and ride good horses and be happy with white-eyed *Hurs* and various kinds of scents and melodies of female slaves together with those other bles-sings; and be exalted in the company of Prophets and *Siddiqs* (perfected men of truth) and *Shahids* (i.e. dedicated witnesses to the cause of truth) and *Salehs* (i.e. ordinary men of piety free from glaring sins) in the high heaven.

THE THIRD DISCOURSE

And he said (may Allah be pleased with him):

When the servant of Allah is in a trial he first tries to escape from it with his own efforts, and when he fails in this he seeks the help of others from among men such as the kings and men of authority, people of the world, men of wealth, and in the case of illness and physical suffering, from physicians and doctors; but if the escape is not secured by these he then turns towards his Creator and Lord the Great and Mighty and app-lies to Him with prayer and humility and praise. So long as he finds the resources in his own self he does not turn towards the people and so long as he finds resources in the people he does not turn towards the Creator.

Further, when he does not get any help from Allah he throws himself in His presence and continues in this state, begg-ing and praying and humbly entreating and praising and submitting his neediness in fear and hope. Allah the Great and Mighty, however, tires him out in his prayer and does not accept it until he is completely disappointed in all the means of the world. The decree of Allah and His work then manifest themselves through him and this servant of Allah passes away from all the worldly means and the activities and efforts of the world and retains just his soul.

At this stage he sees nothing but the work of Allah the Great and Mighty and becomes, of necessity, a believer in the unity of Allah (*Tawhid*) to the degree of certainty, that in reality there is no doer of anything excepting Allah and no mover and stopper excepting Him and not good and no evil and no loss and no gain and no benefit and no conferring and no withholding and no opening and no closing and no death and no life and no honour and no dishonour and no affluence and no poverty but in the hand of Allah.

He then becomes in the presence of Allah as a sucking baby in the hands of its nurse or a dead body in the hands of the person who gives it the funeral bath or a ball before the stick of the polo-player,—kept revolving and rolling and changing position after position and condition after condition and he feels no strength either in his own self or in others besides himself for any movement. He thus vanishes from his own self out into the work of his Master.

So he sees nothing but his Master and His work, and hears and understands nothing excepting Him. If he sees anything it is His work and if he hears and knows anything, he hears His word and knows through His knowledge and he becomes gifted with His gifts and becomes lucky through His nearness and through his nearness he becomes decorated and honoured and becomes pleased and comforted and satisfied with His promise and is drawn towards His word and he feels aversion for and is repelled from those besides Him and he desires and relies on His remembrance and he becomes established in Him, the Great and Mighty, and relies on Him and obtains guidance from, and clothes and dresses himself with, the light of His knowledge and is apprised of the rare points of His knowledge and of the secrets of His power and he hears and remembers only from Him the Great, the Mighty, and then offers thanks and praise therefore and takes to prayer.

THE FOURTH DISCOURSE

Said he (may Allah be pleased with him):

When you are dead to the creation, it will be said to you: "May Allah have mercy on you," and Allah will make you die out of the desires of the flesh. And when you die out of the desires of the flesh it will be said to you: "May Allah have mercy on you." Then He will give you death in your will and desires; and when you are dead in your will and desires it will be said to you: "May Allah have mercy on you," and He will restore you to (a new) life.

Now you will be given a life after which there is no death, and you will be enriched with wealth after which there is no poverty; and you will be awarded a gift after which there will be no obstruction, and you will be made happy with happiness after which there will be no sorrow and misery, and you will be blessed with a blessing after which there will be no adversity; and you will be equipped with knowledge after which there will be no ignorance; and you will be given a security after which there will be no fear; and you will be made to prosper so as not to be unlucky; and will be honoured so as not to be dishonoured; and you will be made near (to Allah) so as not to be kept away; and you will be exalted so as not to be lowered; and you will be honoured so as not to be abused; and you will be purified so as not to be polluted any more; then you will be the fulfilment of all hopes and the (flattering) remarks (of people) will assume reality in your case; you will then become the philosopher's stone so much so that you will elude being recognised (in your elevated position), and you will be so exalted that you will have no like of yourself, unique that you will have no peer and no equal. You will become unique and peerless, most hidden and most secret.

You will then become the successor of every Messenger and Prophet of Allah and every Truthful man (*Siddiq*). You will become the finishing point of all saintliness (*wilayat*) and the living saints will flock to you. And through you will the difficulties be solved and through your prayers will the clouds, rain and the fields yield harvest; through your prayers will be removed the calamities and troubles of the rank and file of people (in the country) of even those living in the frontiers, of the rulers and the subjects, of the leaders and the followers and of all creatures. So you will be the police officer (so to speak) for cities and people.

The people will traverse distances and hasten towards you and they will bring gifts and offerings and render you service, in every condition of life, by the permission of the Creator of things. The tongues of people will (at the same time) be busy everywhere with applause and praise for you. And no two persons of faith will differ with regard to you. O! the best of those who live in populated areas and those who travel about, this is the grace of Allah and Allah is the Possessor of mighty grace.

THE FIFTH DISCOURSE

He (may Allah be pleased with him) said:

When you see the world in the hands of those who are of it, with its decorations and vanities, its deceptions and snares, and its fatal poison of which the outside is soft to touch and the inside injurious and which is quick to destroy and kill whosoever touches it and deceives them with it and keeps them indifferent towards its evils and treacheries and breaches of promises — when you see all this, be like one who sees a man answering the call of nature, exposing his private parts and emitting bad smell thereby. As (in such circumstances) you refrain from looking towards his nakedness and shut your nose from the bad odour and foul smell, similarly you should act towards the world; when you see it, turn away your sight from its tinsels and close your nose against the foul smell of its sensualities and gross enjoyments, so that you may remain safe from it and its trials, while what is appointed as your portion will come to you all right and you will enjoy it. Allah said to His chosen Prophet (peace and blessings of Allah be upon him): "And do not cast your look of greed on what We have given certain classes of them to enjoy of the splendour of this world's life, that We may thereby try them and the sustenance given by your Lord is better and more abiding" (The Holy Qur'an, xx-131).

THE SIXTH DISCOURSE

He (may Allah be pleased with him) said:

Vanish from the people by the command of Allah and from your desire by His order, and from your will by His action, so that you may become fit to be the vessel of the knowledge of Allah. Now the sign of your vanishing from the people is that you should be completely cut off from them and from all social contacts with them and make your mind free from all expectations for what is in their control.

And the sign of your vanishing from your desires is that you should discard all efforts for and contact with worldly means in acquiring any benefit and avoiding any harm and you should not move yourself in your own interest and not rely on yourself in matters concerning yourself and not protect yourself nor help yourself, but leave the whole thing entirely to Allah because He had the charge of it in the beginning and so will He have it till the end, just as the charge rested on Him when you were hidden in the womb (of your mother) as also when you were being suckled as a baby in the cradle.

And the sign of your vanishing from your will by the action of Allah is that you should never entertain any resolve and that you should have no objective, nor should any feeling of need be left in you nor any purpose, because you will not have any objective other than the one of Allah. Instead, the action of Allah will be manifested in you, so that at the time of the operation of the will and act of Allah you will maintain passivity of the organs of your body, calmness of your heart, broadness of your mind, and keep your face shining and your inside flourishing and you will be above the need of things because of your connection with their Creator. The hand of Power will keep you in movement and the tongue of Eternity will be calling you and the Lord of the Universe will be teaching you and will clothe you with light from Himself and with spiritual dress and will install you in the ranks of past men of knowledge.

After this (experience) you will ever remain broken down so that neither any sensual desire nor any will stays in you, like a broken vessel which retains neither any water nor any dreg. And you will be devoid of all human actions so that your inner self will accept nothing but the will of Allah. At this stage miracles and supernatural things will be ascribed to you. These things will be seen as if proceeding from you whereas in fact they will be acts of Allah and His will.

Thus you will be admitted in the company of those whose hearts have been smashed and their animal passions have vanished, whereafter they have been inspired with Divine will and new desires of the daily existence. It is in reference to this stage that the Holy Prophet (peace and blessings of Allah be upon him) says: "Three things out of your world have been made dear to me—perfume, women, and prayer, wherein has been reposed the coolness of my eyes." Indeed things have been ascribed to him after they have first gone out of and vanished from him, as we have already hinted. Allah says, "I an with those who are broken-hearted on account of Me."

So Allah the Exalted will not be with you unless all your desires and your will are smashed. And when they are smashed and nothing is left in you and you are fit for nothing but Him, Allah will create you afresh and will give you a new will-power where with to will. And if in the newly-created will there is found again even the slightest tinge of yourself, Allah the Exalted will break this one also, so that you will always remain broken-hearted. In this way, He will go on creating new wills in you and on yourself being found in it, He will smash it every time, till at last the destiny reaches its end and the meeting (of the Lord) takes place. And this is the meaning of the Divine words: "I am with those who are broken-hearted on My account." And the meaning of our words: "Yourself being found in it" is that you get fixed up and satisfied in your new desires.

Allah says in one of His unofficial revelations to the Holy Prophet (may Allah's peace and blessings be upon him) (called Hadithe Qudsi) : "My faithful servant constantly seeks My nearness through optional prayers till I make him my friend and when I make him my friend, I become his ear with which he hears, and his eyes with which he sees, and his hands with which he holds (things), and his legs with which he walks, i.e. he hears through Me, sees through Me, holds through Me and understands through Me." This is undoubtedly the state of *fana* (or self-annihilation). And when you are annihilated in respect of yourself and the creation and since the creation is good or bad, as you yourself are good or bad, you will be in no expectation of any good from them nor fear any evil from them. All that will be left will be now of Allah alone, as it was before He started creation, and in His ordination lie good and evil.

So He will give you safety from the evil of His creation and will submerge you under the ocean of His good; thus you will become the focussing point of all that is good and the spring-head of all blessings and happiness and pleasure and light and peace and tranquillity. So *fana* or self-annihilation is the aim and object and the final end and base of the journey of the saints. All the previous saints in their different stages of development have been asking for persistent efforts for changing their own will to the will of Allah. All of them unto the end of their life annihilated their own will and transformed it into the will of Allah. This is why they are called *Abdal* (a word derived from *Badala* meaning "change"). Thus in the view of these personages it is a sin to associate their own will with the will of Allah.

And in the event of forgetfulness and overwhelming emotion and fear, Allah the Great comes to their help with His mercy by reminding and awakening them, so that they return from their forgetfulness and seek the protection of their Lord because there is no one absolutely free from the blemish of will excepting the angels. The angels are maintained in the purity of their will and the Prophets are maintained in their freedom from the desires of the flesh and the rest of the creation among the Jinn and the human beings charged with the responsibility of moral behaviour are not protected in either way. Of course, the saints are protected from the desires of the flesh and the *Abdal* from the impurity of will or motive. But even these cannot be regarded as free from these two respective evils because it is possible for them to be inclined towards these two weaknesses at times, but Allah overtakes them with His mercy and brings them to their senses.

THE SEVENTH DISCOURSE

He (Allah be pleased with him) said :

Get out from your own self and be away from it and be a stranger to your sense of self and surrender everything to Allah and become His gatekeeper at the door of your heart and keep His commandments by admitting whomsoever he permits to be admitted and honour His prohibition by keeping out everything which He forbids so as not to allow the desire of the flesh to get into your heart after it has gone out of it. And to expel the desire of the flesh from the heart one has to put up resistance to it and refuse subordination to it in all conditions, and to admit it into the heart means to acknowledge subordination to it and to make alliance with it. So do not will anything which is not the will of Allah. Any will of yours which is not the will of Allah is a desire of the flesh, which is, so to say, the wilderness of the fools and it is death for you and a cause of falling away from the sight of Allah and of screening Him away from yourself, if you are in this wilderness. Always guard the commandment of Allah and abstain from His prohibitions and surrender to Him always in all that He has ordered and do not associate with Him anything from His creation. Thus your will and your desire and your passions are all His creations. So do not will anything nor desire anything nor indulge in any passion so that you may not prove to be a polytheist, Allah says :

"Whoever hopes to meet his Lord he should do good deeds, and not join anyone in the service of his Lord." (xviii-110)

Polytheism consists not merely in idol-worship. It is also polytheism to follow the desire of the flesh and to adopt anything of this world and of the hereafter in association with Allah. Because whatever is, besides Allah is not the Master. Thus when you are engaged in anything which is besides Him you are undoubtedly associating that other thing with Allah. Therefore beware and do not rest, and fear and do not feel secure, seek and do not remain indifferent ; then alone will you attain security. And do not ascribe any condition and position of yours to your own self and do not claim anything among these for yourself. Thus if you are placed in any con-

dition or raised to any position do not speak of it to anyone.
Because in the changing of circumstances from day to day, the
glory of Allah manifests itself in an ever-new aspect : and
Allah intervenes between His servants and their hearts. It may
be that the thing about which you speak may be removed from
you and the thing which you think to be permanent and abiding may undergo a change so that you will be put to shame
before those to whom you spoke about them. You should
rather reserve the knowledge of this within your own self and
should not communicate it to others. Then if the thing continues
in existence know it to be the gift of Allah and ask for power
to be thankful and for an increase in the favours of Allah, But
if the thing ceases to exist it will bring progress in knowledge
and light and wakefulness and regard. Allah says :
    "Whatever communication We abrogate or cause it to be
forgotten, we bring one better than it or like it. Do you not
know it that Allah has power over all things ?" (ii 106).

    So do not consider Allah to be powerless in anything and
do not ascribe any shortcoming to His decree and His procedure and do not entertain doubt about His promise. In this
matter let there be an example for virtuous conduct in the Holy
Prophet of Allah. Verses and chapters that were revealed to
him and were adopted in practice were recited in the mosques
and written in books, even these were taken up and changed
and replaced by others and attention of the Holy Prophet (may
Allah's peace and blessings be upon him) was directed towards
these new revelations which replaced the old ones. This happened in the external law.

    As for the inner things and knowledge and spiritual
state which obtained between him and Allah, he used to say
that his heart used to be clouded and he used to seek the protection of Allah seventy times each day, and it is also narrated
that a hundred times a day the Holy Prophet (may Allah's peace
and blessings be upon him) used to be taken from one condition to another and from this to still another and thus he would
be made to attain higher and higher stages in the nearness of
Allah and stages in his match in the unseen and the robe of
light with which he was clothed used to be changed accordingly,

every progressive step making the previous stage appear dark
and defective in comparison and comparatively faulty in respect
of obedience to the commandments. So he used to receive
instructions for the asking of protection from Allah because
the best of all states in a servant is the state of seeking protection and of turning to Allah. This is because in it there is
acknowledgment of his sin and fault and these are the two
qualities which are found in a servant in all conditions of his
life and which belong to him as a heritage from Adam (peace
be on him) who was the father of mankind and the choosen one
of Allah. When the darkness of forgetfulness to the promise
and covenant besmirched the clearness of his spiritual condition and he manifested the desire to abide in the abode of peace
and in the neighbourhood of the Beneficent and Benevolent
Friend (Allah), and he wished for the coming of honoured angels
to him with blessings and peace, at that time his personal
desire manifested itself and the will of Adam was found mixed
up with the will of Allah. So this will of his was smashed and
the first state was made to disappear and the nearness to Allah
then existing was taken away and his the then position slipped
away from him and the light of faith that was with him was
changed into darkness and the purity of his spirit was thereby
darkened. Then this chosen one of Allah was reminded (of his
fault) and was made to acknowledge his sin and mistake and
was instructed to admit his fault and imperfection.

Then said Adam (peace be on him), "Our Lord! we have
been unjust to our own souls and if Thou will not forgive us
and have mercy on us we shall most surely be among the
losers." Then came to him the light of guidance and the
knowledge of repentance and the knowledge of reality consequent thereon and the knowledge of the wisdom that was hidden
in the incident before this and would not be revealed but for
this incident, then Allah turned towards them mercifully so that
they might repent. Then that purpose of his (Adam's) was
changed for another and his previous condition also and there
came to him the higher state of saintliness (*Wilayat*) and he
was given a station in this world and in the hereafter. Thus
did this world become a living place for him and his progeny
and the hereafter the place for their return and eternal rest.

Thus thou shouldst take the Holy Prophet Muhammad (peace and blessings of Allah be on him) who is His friend and the chosen one, and his great ancestor Adam the chosen of Allah, both of whom were among the friends of Allah, as your example in the confession of your fault and in seeking His protection from sins and in the adoption of humility and meekness in all conditions of life.

THE EIGHTH DISCOURSE

He (may Allah be pleased with him) said:

When you are in a particular condition do not wish for another condition either higher or lower. Thus when you are at the palace gate of the King do not wish for an entrance into the palace unless you are made to enter it by compulsion and not of your own accord. And by compulsion I mean a stern order which is repeated. And do not consider it enough to have the mere permission for entrance, because this may just be a trick and a deception from the King. You should rather hold your patience till you are compelled to enter the house by the sheer force of command from and action of the King. For then you will not be overtaken by any chastisement from the King on account of this action of His own. If, however, you meet with any punishment it will be on account of the evil of your liking and greed and impatience and unmannerliness and want of contentment with the condition of life you were in. Then when it so happens that you enter the palace under such a compulsion, enter it in all silence and with your looks cast down, observing proper manners and being attentive to whatever you are commanded to do by way of any service and occupation, without asking for any promotion in the station of life. Allah said to His Prophet Muhammad, His chosen one (may Allah's peace and blessings be upon him) :

"And do not stretch your eyes after that with which We have provided different classes of them, of the splendour of this world's life, that We may thereby try them ; and the sustenance (given) by your Lord is better and more abiding". (xx-131).

Thus by His words, "The sustenance (given) by your Lord

is better and more abiding," Allah administers an admonition to His Holy Prophet, the chosen one (may Allah's peace and blessings be upon him) to make him regardful of the existing condition and to remain contented with the gifts of Allah. To put this commandment in other words, "Whatever I have given you of good things and prophethood and knowledge and contentment and patience and kingdom of religion and fighting for the sake of religion—all these are better and worthier than what I have given to others". Thus all good lies in being regardful of the existing condition and in being contented with it and in warding off all desires for anything which is besides it, because such a thing must be either one that is allotted to you or one which is allotted to another person or the one which is allotted to nobody, but has been created by Allah as a trial. So if it is destined for you, it is bound to come to you, whether you like it or dislike it. It is not proper, therefore, that any unmannerliness should be manifested from you or any greed in your desire for it, because it is disapproved by the standards of intelligence and knowledge. And if it is destined for another man, why should you bear hardships for a thing which you cannot get and which is never to reach your hands. And if it is a thing which is not to fall to the lot of any man that is only a trial ; how can an intelligent person like and approve that he should ask for himself a trial and actively seek for it ? Thus it is proved that good and safety lies wholly in paying regard to the existing condition. Then when you are made to climb up to the upper storey and from there to the roof of the palace you should observe, as we have already stated, respectfulness, silence and good manners. Nay you should do more than this because you are now nearer the King and closer to dangers. So do not desire any change from your existing state to any other state, higher or lower, nor should you desire either for its continuity and permanence or for any change in it. Nay, you should have no option whatsoever in the matter because that will amount to ingratitude in respect of the existing blessings and such a sense of ingratitude, of necessity, renders him, who is guilty of this, abased in this life and the hereafter. So keep on acting as we have told you, until you are raised to a position where you will be granted a fixed status wherefrom you will not be removed, you should then know that it is a gift of Allah accompanied as it is with the manifestation of its indications and signs. You should, therefore, stick to it and not allow yourself to be removed from it. The *Ahwal* (states of spiritual changes) belong to the *Awliya* (ordinary saints) whereas *Muqamat* (stations of spiritual establishment) to *Abdal* (or advanced saints).

THE NINTH DISCOURSE

He (Allah be pleased with him) said :

Such acts of Allah are manifested to the *Awliya* and the *Abdal* in the course of *Kashf* (spiritual vision) and *Mushahida* (spiritual experiences) as overwhelm the reasoning power of man and shatter into pieces all habits and customs. This manifestation is of two kinds — one of them is called *Jalal* (majesty and glory), and the other *Jamal* (gracefulness). The Jalal produces a disquieting fear and creates a disturbing apprehension and overpower the heart in such an awful manner that its symptoms become visible on the physical body. Thus it is narrated of the Holy Prophet Muhammad (peace and blessings of Allah be upon him) that during prayer a simmer very much like that of a boiling cauldron could be heard from his heart and this on account of the intensity of fear caused by his observing the Majesty of Allah, an experience which also revealed to him His glory. And similar things are reported from Prophet Ibrahim (Abraham) alaihissalam the friend of Allah and Caliph Hazrat Umar (peace of Allah be on both).

The experience of Allah's graceful manifestation, however, is His reflection on the heart of man producing light, joy, elegance and sweet words and loving conversation and glad tidings with regard to great gifts and high position and closeness to Himself, whereto all their affairs are eventually to return, and in the allotment of which in the beginning of time the pen of destiny became dried and which were appointed in the remote past. This is a favour from Him and mercy and a confirmation meant for them is this world till the completion of time which is appointed. This is done so that they may not exceed the limits of appropriate love in the sheer intensity of their desire

for it and thereby their hearts may not break and they meet
with destruction or become weakened by their standing in
servitude till the time there comes to them certainty by which
we mean death. He does this with them just out of kindness
and mercy and regard and also by way of training their hearts
out of affection because He is wise, knowing. gentle towards
them and kind. So it is that it is related of the Holy Prophet
(peace and blessings of Allah be upon him) that he used to say
to Hazrat Bilal (may Allah be pleased with him) who used to
sound the call for prayers : "Cheer our heart, O Bilal." What
he meant was that he should sound the call of prayer so that
the Holy Prophet (may Allah's peace and blessings be upon
him) might enter the state of prayer to experience those graceful manifestations of Allah which we have already discussed.
This is why the Holy Prophet (may Allah's peace and blessings
be upon him) said. "And the coolness of my eyes has been
reposed in prayer."

THE TENTH DISCOURSE

He (Allah be pleased with him) said

Verily there is nothing excepting Allah and your self and
you are the addresser, and the self of man is opposed to Allah
and inimical to Him and all things are subordinate to Allah
and the self of man really belongs to Allah as a creation and as
a possession and the self of man entertains presumptions wherefrom arise false hopes and passions and sensual pleasure. So if
you ally your self with truth by opposing your self and becoming hostile to it you will belong to Allah and become inimical
to your self. Thus Allah said to Prophet Dawood (David)
(peace be on him); "O Dawood (David), I am your unavoidable resort, so hold firmly to this resort ; true servitude consists
in your becoming inimical to your own self for My sake." It
is then that your friendliness towards Allah and servitude of
Him will become a proved fact. And it is then that you will
get your share of things holy, wholesome and pleasant. You
will then become dear and honourable and everything will
become your servant and render you homage and will be afraid
of you, because all of them are subordinate to their Allah and

in harmony with Him, since He is their Creator and Originator and they acknowledge their servitude to Him. Allah says :

"And there is nothing that does not glorify Him with His praises, but you do not understand their prayer".

This means that everything in this universe is conscious of His presence and obeys His commands. And Allah of might and glory said :

Then He said to it and to the world : "Come you both willingly or unwillingly," and they both said : "We come willingly."

Thus all servitude consists in opposing your self and your carnal desires. Allah says :

"Do not follow your low desires because they will lead you astray from the path of Allah. (xxxviii-26)

He has also said :

"Shun your low desires because there is nothing that contends with Me in My kingdom excepting the carnal desire of man."

And there is a famous incident related of Abu Yazid Bustami (may Allah's mercy be upon him) that when he saw Allah the Almighty in his dream, he asked Him, "How is one to get to You ?" Allah said, "Discard yourself and come to Me." "Then," continues the Saint, "I got out of my self as a snake gets out of its slough " Thus all good lies in fighting one's self in everything and in all conditions of life. If, therefore, you are in a state of piety oppose your self so much so that you may keep away from the forbidden things of the people and their doubtful things and from their acts of help and from depending on them and putting any reliance on them or from any fear from them or from coveting what they possess of the vanities of the world. Thus you should not expect any gift from them by way of present or alms or charity or by way of redemption for certain lapses in a fulfilment of some vow. You should, therefore, free your self from all concern about the means of the world in all their various aspects so much so that if you have got a relation who is wealthy do not desire his death with a view to inheriting his wealth. Thus you should get out of the creation with a strenuous effort and consider them like a gate that closes and opens and like a tree which sometimes yields fruit and at other times remains barren and (know that) every such event is the doing of a doer and planned by a planner and He is Allah, so that you may be believer in the oneness of Allah.

And do not forget at the same time the position of human efforts so as not to fall a victim to the creed of the fatalists (Jabariyya), and believe that no action attains its fulfilment but in Allah, the Exalted. You should not, therefore, worship them and thus forget Allah nor should you say that the actions of men proceed from anything but from Allah because if you say so you will become an unbeliever and belong to the category of people known as Qad-riya (believers in the doctrine that men have absolute control over the origin and cause of actions). You should rather say that actions belong to Allah in points of creation and to men in point of effort, and this is the view that has been handed down to us by traditions which relate to the discussion on rewards and punishments.

And execute the commandment of Allah pertaining to them (people) and set apart your own share from them by His commandment and do not exceed this limit because the order of Allah will stand and it will judge you as well as them; do not be the judge yourself. And your being with them (people) is a decree of Allah and this decree of Allah is in darkness, so enter this darkness with a lamp which is also the judge and this is the Book of Allah and the practice of His Holy Prophet (may Allah's peace and blessings be upon him). Do not go beyond these two. But if there arises in your mind any thought or you receive any revelation, submit them before the Book of Allah and the practice of His Holy Prophet (may Allah's peace and blessings be upon him).

And if you find in these (authorities) a prohibition against what has occurred to you or been received by you through revelation, such as if it is revealed to you that you should commit fornication or take to usury or keep company with immoral people or something else in the line of sinfulness, keep away from such a course of action and abstain from it and do not accept it and do not act upon it and remain firm in your

conviction that this must be from devil the accursed and if you
find in these two authorities just an allowance for the things
revealed to you such as fulfilment of lawful desires like eating,
drinking, dressing or marrying, etc. abstain from it likewise and
do not accept it and know that it is a suggestion of your animal
self and its desires and that you are commanded to oppose it
and be hostile to it.

And if you find in the Book of Allah and in the practice of
the Holy Prophet (may Allah's peace and blessings be upon him)
neither any prohibition nor a mere permission for the thing
received through revelation but is a thing which you cannot
understand, such for instance as that you are asked to go to a
certain place or meet such and such a righteous person whereas
through the blessings of Allah bestowed on you in the form of
knowledge and illumination you do not stand in need of going
to that place or meeting the person mentioned, hold your
patience in the matter and do not be in any hurry about it, so
as to ask yourself: "Is it a revelation from Allah and should I
act upon it?" Rather wait to decide on any step in the matter.
And it is a practice of Allah of power and glory to repeat such a
revelation and to command you to be quick in your efforts in
the matter or to reveal such a sign which is revealed to the
people of knowledge of Allah—a sign which is understandable
only by the intelligent among the *Awliya* and the confirmed
among the *Abdal*, and you should by no means be in any hurry
about the matter because you do not know the sequel of the
matter and the ultimate purpose of the affair, nor are you
aware of where lies a trial and a path of ruin, and a subtle
planning contrived by Allah and an examination for you.

So you should be patient till Allah Himself becomes the doer
of the thing in you. So when the act becomes distinctively of
Allah and you are carried to such a position, if now any trial
confronts you, you will be safely carried through it because
Allah the Exalted will not chastise you for an action which is
His own and it is certain that chastisement comes to you for
your active participation in the happening of a thing.

And if you are in the state of reality and it is the state of
Wilayat (saintliness), then stand opposed to *your* passions and
obey the commandments fully. And obedience to command-

ments is of two kinds. One is that you should take from
the world means of subsistence to the extent of the just demands
of yourself and that you should avoid indulging in sensual
pleasures and perform your duties and engage yourself in
warding off sins, open and secret. And the second kind relates
to the hidden commandment; and it is the commandment of
Allah with which He either enjoins His servant to do or forbids
him doing anything. And this hidden commandment applies to
things permissible, for which there is no positive injunction in
the Law, in the sense that they neither belong to the class of
prohibited things, nor to the class of things specified as
obligatory, but are rather of an obscure nature wherein the
servant is given complete freedom to act, and these are called
Mubah. In these the servant should not take any initiative,
but wait for an order concerning them. When he receives an
order he obeys it. Thus all his movements and restful conditions become dedicated to Allah. If there is an injunction in Law
with regard to a certain thing, he acts in accordance with it, but
if there is no injunction in the Law, he acts on the hidden commandment. It is through these that he becomes confirmed as a
man attaining reality.

And where there is not (even) this hidden commandment,
and is just an act of Allah, it entails a state of resignation. And
if you have attained the truth of truth which is otherwise called
the state of immersion (*mahw*) or annihilation (*fana*) it is the
state of the *Abdal*—who are broken-hearted on account of Him,
a state belonging to pure monotheists, to men of spiritual
enlightenment; to men of knowledge and (higher) intelligence.
(who are) chief of the chiefs, the wardens and protectors of
people, the vicegerents of the Beneficent, and His friends and
confidants, peace be on them. To pay obedience to the commandment in such matters is to go against your own self and
to be free from reliance on any ability and power and to be
absolutely devoid of all will and purpose with regard to anything
of this world and the hereafter. Thus you will become the
servant of the King, and not of the Kingdom, of Divine commandment and not of the desires of the flesh and will become
like a baby in the care of a nature or a dead body at the
time of funeral wash in the hands of the washer or an unconscious.

patient lying before the physician, in all matters that are outside
the range of injunctions and prohibition.

THE ELEVENTH DISCOURSE

Said he (may Allah be pleased with him):

When the desire for marriage arises in your mind while
you are poor and needy and you find yourself unable to afford
it and you hold yourself in patience in expectation of relief
from Allah whose power created in you such a desire, or
who found the desire in you, He Himself will help you (either
by removing the desire from you) or sustain you in bearing the
burden of the same by making its resources accessible to you
by way of gift, together with His blessings for sufficiency and
making it light for you in this world and easy in the other. Then
Allah will call you patient and grateful because of your patience
in the matter and contentment with His Providence. So He will
increase you in purity and power. And if it is a decree of
Providence towards which He has driven you with His blessings
of sufficiency, your patience will change into gratitude and the
Mighty and Glorious has promised the grateful ones increase in
His gifts, as He says:

"If you are grateful, I would certainly give you more, and
if you are ungrateful, My chastisement is truly severe". (xiv-7)

And if it is not destined for you, you should be indifferent
towards it, and drive it away from your heart whether your
animal self likes it or not. You should thus hold your patience
and oppose your desire and hold fast to the commandment of
the Law. Be contented with the decree of Providence and hope
in this condition for the favour and gift of Allah. Indeed
Allah Himself has said :

"Only the patient will be paid back their reward in full
without measure."

THE TWELFTH DISCOURSE

Said he (Allah be pleased with him) :

When Allah the Mighty and Glorious gives you wealth
and you are diverted by it from obedience to Him, He screens

you away, on account of it from Himself both in this world as well as in the hereafter. And it is also possible that He may take away the gift from you and change you and reduce you to poverty as a punishment for your turning away from the Giver, attracted by the gift. And if you engage yourself with obedience to Him and become indifferent towards the wealth, Allah will make a free gift of it to you and will not lessen it even by an atom. Wealth is your servant and you are the servant of the Lord. Therefore live in this world under His loving care and in the hereafter honourably and in ease in the garden of abiding residence, in the company of the truthful (*Siddiqs*) and witnesses (*Shahids*) and the virtuous (*Salihs*).

THE THIRTEENTH DISCOURSE

Said he (Allah be pleased with him) :
Do not make any effort to appropriate any blessing, nor to ward off any calamity. The blessing will come to you if it is destined for you, whether you seek it or dislike it. And the calamity will overtake you if it is destined for you, whether you dislike it and try to ward it off by prayer or confront it with your patience and fortitude in order to earn the pleasure of the Lord.

You should surrender yourself in everything so that He may do His work through you. If it be a blessing be engaged in thanksgiving and if it be a calamity either exhibit patience or try to cultivate patience and alliance with Allah and His pleasure or try to feel His blessing in this or be merged in Him through this as far as you can afford, by means of spiritual states which are given to you, and in which you are being turned over again and again and in which you are made to journey from stage to stage in your way towards Allah to obey and befriend whom you are commanded, so that you may meet the Great Friend (Allah).

You will then be made to stand at a place which has been reached before by the *Siddiqs* and *Shahids* and *Salihs*. That is to say you will attain to extreme nearness to Allah so that you may observe the position of those who have gone before you to the heavenly King, the Lord of Glory and Mighty Kingdom,

and who have attained nearness to Him and received from Him
every kind of amenity and joy and security and honour and
blessing. And let the calamity visit you and do not obstruct its
way nor confront it with your prayer nor feel uneasy over its
coming and approaching you, because its fire is not more terri-
ble than the fire of Hell in flames.

It is reliably related in the traditions about the best of
mankind and the best of those whom the earth carries on its
surface and the sky covers with its shade. I mean the Prophet
Muhammad (the chosen one) that he said :

"Verily the fire of Hell will speak to the believer saying,
Pass hurriedly alone O believer, because your light is extinguish-
ing my flame".

Now, is not the light of a believer which extinguishes the
flame of Hell the same which is to be found with him in this
world and which distinguishes those who obey Allah from
those who disobey ? Let the same light extinguish the flame
of calamity and let the coolness of your patience and harmony
with Allah extinguish the heat of what is going to overtake you.

Thus the calamity has not come to you to crush you but
to try you and to confirm the correctness of your faith and to
strengthen the foundation of your convictions and to give you
inwardly the good news from your Lord about His kind
thoughts for you. Allah says :

"And most certainly We will try you until We have known
those among you who exert themselves hard, and the patient
and made your case manifest (xlvii-31)".

Thus when your faith with Allah is proved and you have
been quite in harmony with His work with certainty, and all
this with the help of power given by Him and of His benevolent
help, then you should always remain patient and in complete
harmony with Him and in fullest obedience to Him. Do not
allow anything to happen in yourself nor in others which may
go against the commandments and prohibitions of Allah. And
when any of His commandments comes, listen to it with attention and be quick to act upon it and be on the move and do
not remain inactive, and do not remain passive before the
decree of Providence and its act but employ your power and
efforts to fulfil the commandment.

Then if you find yourself unable to carry out the order do not lose time in repairing to Allah. Seek His refuge and humble yourself before Him and ask His forgiveness and try to find out the cause of your inability to carry out His order and to be prevented from being honoured by your obedience to Him. Possibly this inability is due to the evil of your presumptions or to your unmannerliness in the course of your obedience to Him or to your pride or to your reliance on your own resources and powers or to your being conscious of your own action or to your associating your own self or the creation with Him, as a result of which He has kept you away from His door and dismissed you from obedience to Him and from His service and shut out from you the help of His strength and turned away from you His benign face and become angry with you and estranged from you and kept you occupied with your trials of the world and with your passions and your vice and your desire. Do you not know that all these things make you oblivious of your Lord and make you fall away from the sight of Him Who has created you and nourished you and blessed you with so many gifts. Beware lest these things which are besides Allah should divert you from your Lord. Everything which is not Allah is besides Allah. So do not accept any other thing in preference to Him, because He has created you for His own sake. So do not be unjust to your own soul so as to be preoccupied with things other than His commandments, because that will cause you to enter the fire, of which the fuel will be the men and the stones and then you will be sorry, but your sorrow will not benefit you and you will make excuses but no excuse will be accepted and you/will cry for help but no help will be forthcoming and you will try to please Allah but without any success and you will try to come back to the world to take stock of experiences and to mend matters but you will not be allowed to return.

Take pity on your soul and be kind to it and bring into use all the instruments for the service of your Lord, such as your intelligence and faith and spiritual enlightenment and knowledge which have been given to you : and seek to illumine your surrounding with the light proceeding from these in the midst of the darkness of destiny and hold fast to the injunctions and prohibitions of Allah and traverse, under the direction provided by these two, the path towards your Lord and surrender whatever is besides these two to Him Who has created you and caused you to grow and do not be ungrateful to Him Who has created you from dust and then from a small life germ then He made you a perfect man. And do not wish for anything which is besides His commandment and do not consider anything bad unless it be His prohibition. Remain contented with regard to this world and the hereafter with the former object in view. And despise, with regard to both of them the latter. Thus everything that may be desired by you should be subservient to the former object and everything despised should be subordinated to the latter hateful thing. When you are in harmony with His commandment the whole universe will pay its homage to you and when you despise the things prohibited by Him all unseemly things will run away from you wheresoever you may happen to remain. Allah has said in some of His books :

"O children of Adam, I am Allah ; there is no other deity besides Me. I say to a thing "be" and it comes to exist. Obey Me ; I will make you such that you will say to a thing "be" and it will be there".

And He also said :

"O earth, whosoever serves Me, serve him and whoever serves you keep him worried".

So when His prohibition comes you should become like one who has become loose and tired in his joints and has lost all physical reactions,—a man with a bruised heart, contracted breast and spiritless body without any desire and purpose, freed from all impressions of the material world, cut off from all and devoid of all signs of animal life and marks of animal desires, like a dark courtyard and a dilapidated, uninhabited building with its roof fallen down, without any perception and any traces of animal existence. You should become like one who is deaf even from his birth and your eyes should be like that of a person who is blindfolded and born blind and your lips should be as if they are full of sores and are swollen and your tongue should be as if it is dumb and coarse and your teeth sould be as if they have pus in their roots and are full of pain and disintegrated and your two hands should be as if they are paralysed and incapable of holding anything and your feet should be as if they are stricken and trembling and full of wounds and your sex organ should be as if it has lost all power and is engaged in other things and your stomach should be as if it is full and indifferent to food, and your understanding as if it is mad and your body should be as if it is dead and carried to the grave.

So you should listen and carry out quickly the commandments of Allah just as you should feel lazy and hesitant and slothful in matters of prohibition and behave like a dead man and be resigned to the decree of Allah. So drink this syrup and take this remedy and have this diet so that you may be free from the desires of the flesh, be cured of the diseases of sin and be free from the bondage of desires and thus be restored to perfect spiritual health.

THE FOURTEENTH DISCOURSE

He (Allah be pleased with him) said :
O you slave of your passions ! do not claim for yourself the position of the people of Allah. You serve your passions and they are worshippers of the Lord. Your desire is the world and the desire of these people is the hereafter. You see this world and they see the Lord of the earth and the Heaven. Your comfort lies in the creation and the comfort of these people lies in Allah. Your heart is bound with what is in this earth and the hearts of these people with the Lord of Divine throne. You are the victim of whatever you see and they do not see what you see, but they see the Creator of the things, who cannot be seen (by these eyes). These people achieve the object of their life and secure salvation for themselves, whereas you remain pawned to your desires of this world.

These people vanish from the creation and from their desires of the world and their wishes and thus they secure an access to the Great Master who gives them strength to achieve the end of their existence such as obedience and praise of the Lord. This is the favour of Allah ; He gives it to whomsoever He likes. They make this obedience and praise incumbent on

themselves and persevere therein with the help of the strength
and ease, given by Him without experiencing any hardship.
Thus obedience becomes their soul and food so to speak.

Accordingly, world becomes a blessing and an enjoyable
thing for them, as if it is a veritable heaven. Because when
they see anything, before they see it they see behind it the act
of Him who has created them. These people thus supply the
staying power to the earth and the heaven and comfort to the
dead and the living, because their Lord has made them like pegs
for the earth which He has spread. Thus everyone of them is
like a mountain which stands firm. So keep away from their
path and do not stand in the way of these people whom their
parents and children have not been able to divert from their
purpose. These people are the best among those whom the
Lord has created and spread in the world ; peace of Allah be
upon them and His greetings and blessings as long as the earth
and the heaven last.

THE FIFTEENTH DISCOURSE

He (Allah be pleased with him) said :

I saw in a dream as if I am in a place like a mosque in which
there are some people who have kept aloof from the rest of
humanity. I said to myself, "If so and so were present here
he could have disciplined these people and given them proper
guidance, etc.," and I thought of a certain man of virtue. These
people gathered round me and one of them said to me, "What
is the matter with you ? Why do you not speak ?" I said,
"If you are pleased with me, I will." Then I said : "When you
have stood aloof from the people for the sake of truth, do not
ask people for anything with your tongue. And when you
have stopped asking so, do not even think of asking anything from them either, because even the thought of asking
is as good as asking with tongue. Then know that Allah
is every day in a new state of glory in changing and altering
and raising and lowering (people). Thus He raises some
people to the highest of heaven and He lowers others to the
lowest depth of degradation. Then He threatens those He
has raised to the highest of Heavens that He may lower them

down to the lowest depth of degradation and gives them the
hope that He will keep them and preserve them in the same
state of exaltation, whereas He threatens those whom He has
thrown to the lowest depth of degradation that He may leave
them to abide in their abasement and holds out the hope to
them that He may raise them to the highest of heavens." Then
I woke up.

THE SIXTEENTH DISCOURSE

He (Allah be pleased with him) said :

Nothing keeps you off from the favour of Allah and His
direct blessing excepting your reliance on people and means and
arts and crafts and earnings. Thus people become a barrier
for you in getting to the livelihood sanctified by the practice
of the Holy Prophet (may Allah's peace and blessings be upon
him) viz. the earning. Thus so long as you remain with people
that is, you hope for their gifts and favours and ask from them
with expectations at their doors, you are associating Allah's
creation with Him. You will accordingly be punished with the
deprivation from a livelihood which is sanctioned by the
practice of the Holy Prophet viz. lawful earnings of this world.

Then when you have renounced yonr living with the people
and your associating them with your Lord and have recourse to
earning and you begin living on your earning and then rely on
earning and become contented with it and forget the favour of
your Lord, you are again behaving like a polytheist and this
polytheism is subtler then the pevious one; so Allah will punish
you and keep you away from His favour and His direct dealing
with you.

Then when you have turned away from this position and
have thrown away polytheism from your midst and discarded
your reliance on your earning, ability and power and you have
seen Allah that He is the Giver of livelihood and Creator of
causes of ease and Giver of strength for earning and Giver of
power over everything good and that livelihood is in His hand,
—sometimes He brings it to you through people by way of your
asking from them at times of trial and struggle or through
your asking from Him, the Mighty and Glorious, and at others

through your earning by way of remuneration and at still others
through His spontaneous favour in such a way that you do not
see the intervening cause and means.

Thus you turn towards Him and throw yourself before Him,
the Mighty, the Glorious, when He lifts the veil that intervenes
between you and His favour and opens the door of sustenance
by His favour at every time of necessity, in proportion to the
need of your circumstances in the manner of a loving physician
who is also a friend to the patient—and this as a protection
from Him, the Mighty, the Glorious, and in order to keep you
clean from any inclination towards what is besides Him and He
thus pleases you by His favour.

Thus when He removes from your heart every purpose and
every desire and every pleasure and every object, there remains
nothing in your heart excepting His purpose. Thus when He
wants to bring to you your allotted share which cannot escape
from you and which is not meant for anyone else from among
His creation, He will create in you a desire for that share and
will direct it to you so it will reach you at the time of your
need. Then He will give you strength to be grateful to Him
and will give you the knowledge that it is from Him and He
will direct it to you and give it to you as your sustenance so
that you may be grateful to Him and my recognise and know it.
Thus this will increase your desire for aloofness from people
and distance from men and emptiness of your heart from whatever is besides Him.

Then when your knowledge has been strengthened, as
also your certainty, and your heart has expanded and is
illumined and your nearness to Allah and your position
with Him and your trustworthiness and worthiness in the matter
of guarding His secrets have been increased thereby, you will
be given knowledge beforehand as to when your share will come
to you as a sign in your favour and as an exaltation of your
dignity. This is a favour from Him, and an act of kindness and
a guidance. Allah says:

"And We made it a guide for the children of Israel. And
We made of them leaders to guide by Our command when they
were patient and they were certain of Our communications."
(xxxii-24).

And He also says :
"And (as for) those who strive hard for Us, We will most certainly guide them in Our ways," (xxix-69).
And Allah, the Exalted and Glorious also says:
And fear Allah and He will teach you, then He will invest you with the power of controlling the universe, with a clear permission, which will have no obscurity in it and with clear signs which will be bright like the bright sun and with sweet words which will be sweeter than all sweet things and with true revelation without any ambiguity and will be free from any evil suggestion of the animal self and from the promptings of the devil, the accursed." Allah says in one of His books:
"O child of Adam, I am Allah, nothing deserves to be worshipped excepting Me. I say to a thing "be" and it comes into being. Obey Me, I will make you such that if you say to a thing "be" it will likewise come into being." And He has done like this with many of his Prophets and *Awliya* and people specially favoured from among the children of Adam.

THE SEVENTEENTH DISCOURSE

He (Allah be pleased with him) said:
When you are united with Allah and you attain His nearness by His attraction and help; and the meaning of union with Allah is your going out of the creation and desire and purpose and becoming established in His action and His purpose without there being any movement in you or through you in His creation unless it be with His order and action and command. So this is the state of *Fana* (annihilation) by which is meant union with Allah. But union with Allah, the Mighty, the Glorious, is not like union with anything in His creation, in an understandable and appointed manner:
"Nothing is like unto a likeness to Him and He is the Hearing, the Seeing." (xlii-11)
The Creator is above being similar to His creatures or bearing any resemblance to anything that He has made. Thus union with Him is a thing which is well known to people, having this experience of union, because of their realisation of it. Everyone of them has a different experience in this matter

which is peculiar to himself and which cannot be shared by any other person.

With everyone among the Prophets and Messengers and the Saints (*Awliya*) of Allah is to be found a secret which cannot be known by any other person, so much so that sometimes it so happens that the *Murid* (spiritual pupil or disciple) holds a secret which is not known to the *Shaikh* (the spiritual preceptor); and sometimes the *Shaikh* holds a secret which is not known to the *Murid* though the latter may in his spiritual journey have approached the very threshold of the door of the spiritual state of his *Shaikh* When the *Murid* reaches the spiritual state of the *Shaikh*, he is made to separate himself from the *Shaikh* and he is cut off from him and Allah becomes his guardian and He cuts him off from the creation altogether.

Thus the *Shaikh* becomes like a wet nurse who has stopped suckling the baby after two years. No connection remains with the creation after the disappearance of low desires and human purpose. The *Shaikh* is needed by him so long as he is infested with low desires and purposes which have to be crushed. But after the disappearance of these weaknesses of the flesh there remains no need of the *Shaikh* because there remains no stain and no defect in the *Murid*.

Thus when you unite with Allah as we have described, you will feel safe for ever from whatsoever is besides Him. You will certainly see no existence at all besides His. Either in profit or in loss or in gifts or with their withholding, in fear or in hope, you will only find Him, the Mighty, the Glorious, who is worthy to be feared and worthy to be sought protection from. So you keep on looking at His acts for ever and expecting His order and remain engaged in obedience to Him, cut off from the whole of His creation whether of this world or of the here-after. Let not your heart be attached to anything in His creation

Consider the whole creation as a man who has been arrested by a King with a great kingdom, strong command, awe-striking might and power, then as if the same King has fettered him neck and legs and then crucified him on a pine tree on the bank of a big river, with huge waves and of great width and depth, and strong in current, and as if then the same King sits on a big throne of great height which it is difficult to reach and the King is armed heavily with arrows and spears and bows and various kinds of weapons of which a true estimate cannot be made by any but himself ; then as if he starts throwing towards the crucified man anything that he likes from among those weapons. Can anyone admire a person who sees all these and then turns away his sight from the King and becomes devoid of fear from him and hope from him and fears instead the man crucified and hopes from him ? Will not the man who does this be called in the judgment of intelligence a foolish man; lacking comprehension, a lunatic, and a brute and inhuman ?

So seek the protection of Allah from being blind after having possessed sight and from being separated after being united and from being taken afar after being near and from going astray after having received guidance and from unbelief after having believed.

"Thus the world is like the great river, flowing on, to which we have referred. Every day its water increases and it is the animal passion of mankind and the enjoyments which come to them from it. As for the arrows and various weapons, they are the trials which destiny brings to them. Thus the predominant elements in the worldly life of man is the trials and hardships and the sufferings and the struggles. And what they get as blessing and enjoyments is also guarded or surrounded by calamities.

When any intelligent man takes a critical view of the matter, if of course he possesses a certain knowledge of the reality, he will understand that there is no real life excepting the life hereafter. Thus the Holy Prophet (may Allah's peace and blessings be upon him) has said : "There is no life excepting the life of the hereafter."

This is particularly true in the case of a believer. Accordingly the Holy Prophet (on him be blessings and peace of Allah) has said

"The world is a prison for the believer and a heaven for the unbeliever."

And he (on him be blessings and peace of Allah) has also. said : "The man of virtue is bridled."

How can a comfortable life in this world be possible and
desired in face of this ? Thus, real comfort lies in a complete
and exclusive contact with Allah, the Mighty and Glorious,
and in being in harmony with Him and in throwing oneself in
absolute surrender before Him. When you do this you will
be free from this world and then will be lavished on you compassion and comfort and kindness and prosperity and favour
of Allah.

THE EIGHTEENTH DISCOURSE

He (may Allah be pleased with him) said
It is a parting advice of mine that you should never complain about any mishap that may befall you to anyone whether
it be a friend or a foe and should not blame your Lord for
what He does to you, and for His causing the trial for you.
You should rather give publicity to what good happens to be
with you and to your thankfulness on that account. Your
telling a lie in expression of your gratitude without any blessing
is better than your stating a true fact and giving publicity to
any grievance for your external circumstances. Who is there
that is devoid of the blessings of Allah ? Allah the Mighty
and Glorious says
"And if you count the blessings of Allah you will not be
able to enumerate them (xiv-34)".
How many blessings there are with you and you do not
recognise them ! Do not feel comforted with anything in the
creation and do not be in love with it and do not communicate
to anyone the state of your affairs. Your love should rather
be for the sake of Allah, the Mighty, the Glorious, and your
comfort should be in him and your grievance against Him
should be communicated only to Him.
You should look to nobody else, because in nothing else
there is any harm or good or any appropriation and renunciation or any honour or dishonour or any elevation or fall or any
poverty or affluence or any movement or pause. All things
are the creation of Allah and in the hand of Allah lies the
source of their movement by His command and permission.
They continue to exist up to a time appointed by Him. And

everyting exists according to a measure fixed by Him. Whatever He has made posterior can by no means be prior and
whatever He has made prior can by no means be made posterior. If Allah intends any harm to you no one can avert it
excepting He. And if He intends any good, no one can with-
hold His favour.

Thus if you complain against Him while you are in comfort
and enjoying some blessings, just desiring an increase in them
and shutting your eyes to what is with you of blessing and
comfort, considering them very poor, Allah will be angry with
you and take these two things away from you and make your
complaint real and double your trouble and intensify His
chastisement and anger and hatred for you ; and He will make
you fall off in His sight.

Therefore, beware of complaint with utmost effort even if
your flesh be cut into pieces by means of scissors. Save yourself ! Fear Allah ! Fear Allah ! Fear Allah ! Make good your
escape ! Make good your escape ! Beware ! Beware !

Verily most of the various calamities that befall the son of
Adam are due to complaint against his Lord. How can one
complain against Him, and He is the most merciful of the
merciful ones and the best of all judges, Patient, Aware Com-
passionate, Merciful, Kind towards His servant ; He is not
unjust to His servants and is like a patient, affectionate, loving,
kind, physician who is also a kinsman (to the patient). Can
any fault be found in an affectionate kind-hearted father or
mother ?

The Holy Prophet (Peace and blessings of Allah be upon
him) has said :

"Allah is more merciful towards His servant than a mother
is towards her son".

O poor man ! show the utmost of good manners. Exhibit
patience at the time of calamity, even if you become exhausted
by patience. Hold on to patience even if you get exhausted
hrough your cheerful submission to and harmony with Allah.
Hold on to cheerful resignation to and concord with Him.
Still remain pleased and get reconciled.

If you are still found in existence vanish out of it. When
you are thus lost, O, you philosopher's stone ! where will you

48   FUTUH AL-GHAIB

be obtained ? Where will you be fcund ? Have you not heard
the word of Allah :
    "Fighting is enjoined on you and it is an object of dislike
to you ; and it may be that you dislike a thing while it is good
for you and it may be that you love a thing while it is bad for
you, and Allah knows and you do not know." (ii-216).
    The knowledge of the reality of things has been kept rolled
away from you and you have been screened away from it. So
do not show bad manners in disliking or liking it. Follow the
Law in all that may happen to you if you are in a state of
piety (*Salih*) which is the first step, and follow the commandment
in the state of *Wilayat* and in the state of dying out of the
existence of desire and do not go beyond this and this is the
second step. And be pleased with the action of Allah and be
reconciled to it and vanish into the state of *Abdal* and *Ghauth*
and *Siddiq* and these are the final stages. Keep clear out of the
way of destiny and do not stand in its way and turn yourself
and your desire, and restrain your tongue from complaint.
    Then when you have done this if the destiny is good, your
Lord will give you more good, and an enjoyable and happy life.
And if it be a bad one Allah will protect you in the course of
it through your obedience to Him and will keep away from you
all blame and will keep you lost in it until the time it passes
away from you and the point of the ripeness of time also
passes ; just as the night passes into the day and the coldness of
winter passes and merges into the summer. Here is an example
for you and you should take lesson from it.
    Again in the self of man there are various kinds of sins and
faults and blemishes on account of which he is unworthy of the
company of Allah, unless he becomes purged of impurities of
sins ; and no one can kiss His threshold except those who are
purified from the dirt of self-conceit, just as no one can be
worthy of the company of kings except those who are cleansed
of impurities and bad smell and dirt. Thus the calamities are
atonements and purifiers. The Holy Prophet (peace and blessings of Allah be upon him) has said : "The fever of cne day is
an atonement for the sins of a whole year."

THE NINETEENTH DISCOURSE

He (may Allah be pleased with him) said :

While you are weak in faith, certainly if a promise is made to you it is fulfilled and it is not broken lest your faith should be diminished thereby or your certainty vanish. But when this faith and certainty is strengthened and established in your heart and you are addressed by His word :

"Verily to-day you are in Our presence an honourable, a faithful one" (*The Holy Qur'an*, xii-54).

And this address is repeated for you many times then you become among the selected ones, rather the select among the selected ones, and there does not remain any will of yours nor any purpose nor any action which you like nor any nearness which you notice nor any position which you may covet and your ambition rises towards it.

Then you become like a vessel with a hole in which no liquid can stay, so that no purpose and habit and no determination for anything of this world or of the other can stay in you and you become cleansed from everything which is besides Allah, the Mighty, the Glorious, and you are enable to be pleased with Allah and you are promised the pleasure of Allah with you and you will be enabled to enjoy and feel blessed with all the actions of Allah.

Then you will be given a promise and when you feel satisfied with it and any sign of will is found in you, you are transferred from this promise towards another which is higher than this. and you are turned towards one which is more honourable and. you are rewarded with a feeling of self-sufficiency with regard to the first and the doors of knowledge will be opened unto you and you will be enlightened on the mysteries of Divine affairs and the truth of wisdom and the deeper purpose in changing the previous promise into the one which followed and' in your new position you will experience an increase in the preservation of (your spiritual) state (*Ha'al*).

Further, you will be granted a spiritual rank wherein you will be entrusted with the preservation of secrets and you will experience an increase in the expansion of your breast and enlightenment of your heart and the eloquence of your tongue and high degree of knowledge and love instilled in your heart. Thus you will be made a beloved of all people and of both men and the Jinn and those besides them in this world and the hereafter. When you become the beloved of Allah, the people are subordinate to Allah and their love is included in His love just as their hatred is included in His hatred.

And so you are made to attain this rank wherein you will have no desire for anything at all.

After this you will be made to desire for something and your desire for that thing will be removed and made to disappear and you will be turned away from it. Thus you will not be given that thing in this world and will be given in the hereafter something in its place which will increase your nearness to Allah, the Great, and that something will cool your eyes in high heaven and the abode of paradise.

And if you have not asked for it nor hoped for it nor inclined towards it while in this world's life which is a place of transitoriness and sufferings but the desire which you did cherish while in this world's life and was your object and purpose and goal was that Being who creates and manifests and withholds and gives and has spread this earth and has held the sky high,—if you have done so you will also be given something in this world's life which will be equivalent to it or may be inferior to it after your heart has been broken by turning you away from that object and goal and after the establishment in the after-life of the thing which you will be given in exchange and which we have already described.

THE TWENTIETH DISCOURSE

He (may Allah be pleased with him) said:

There is a saying of the Holy Prophet Muhammad (peace and blessings of Allah be upon.him):

"Discard whatever creates any doubt with regard to lawfulness and unlawfulness of a thing in your mind and adopt what does not cause any doubt in you."

When a doubtful thing becomes mixed up with a non-doubtful thing, adopt the course in which there is no tinge of any doubt and suspicion and discard what causes any doubt.

But when it is the case of a doubtful thing which is not free from hesitation and a consequent disturbance of mind such as is narrated in a tradition of Prophet Muhammad (peace and blessings of Allah be upon him)—"Sin creates disturbance in the heart"—wait in a case like this for the inner command. Then if you are commanded to adopt it, do as you like. And if you are forbidden, then refrain and let the thing be to you as if it had never been and never existed and turn towards the door of Allah and seek from Him your sustenance.

If you feel exhausted with patience and concord and cheerful surrender and immersion (*Fana*), remember that He, the Mighty and Glorious, does not stand in need of being reminded, and He is not forgetful of you and others besides you; He the Mighty, the Glorious, feeds the unbelievers and the hypocrites and those who have turned away from His obedience. Now is it possible that He would forget you, O, you believer, who believe in His oneness, and persist in your obedience to Him and are firm in carrying out His orders day and night.

Another saying of the Holy Prophet (may peace and blessings of Allah be upon him) namely, "Discard what raises doubt in your mind and adopt what does not raise any," means that you should leave what is in the hands of people and not seek it and should not set your heart at it and not expect anything from people nor fear them and should receive from the favour of Allah and this is what will not cause you any doubt.

Let, therefore, be only one from whom to ask and one giver and one purpose and this should be your Lord, the Mighty, the Glorious, in whose hands lie the forehead (fate) of kings and hearts of people which are again the kings of bodies—that is to say the hearts have the control of the bodies—the bodies and the money of the people belong to Him and the people are His agents and trustees and when they give you anything the movement of their hands is by His permission and command and His motion and same is the case of any gift being withheld from you.

Allah the Mighty says: "Ask from Allah His favour" (iv-32). He also says: "Surely those whom you serve besides Allah do not control for you any sustenance; therefore seek the sustenance

from Allah and serve Him and be grateful to Him." He also
has said: "When My servants ask thee concerning Me surely I
am very near; I accept the prayer of a praying one when he
prays to Me." He also says: "Call upon Me and I will answer
you (xl-60)." He also says: "Surely Allah is the Bestower of
sustenance, the Lord of power, the strong." Still further He
says: "Surely Allah provides sustenance to whom He pleases
without measure."

THE TWENTY-FIRST DISCOURSE

He (may Allah be pleased with him) said:
"I saw Satan the accursed in a dream as if I was in a big
crowd and I intended to kill him. Then he said to me "Why are
you going to kill me and what is my sin? If providence sets the
evil in motion I have no power to change it and transform it
into good. And if providence sets the good in motion I have no
power to change and transform it into evil. And what is there
in my hand?" And I found his appearance resembling that of a
eunuch, soft in speech, a line of hairs fringing his chin, miserable
looking and ugly faced, as if he was smiling before me, full of
shame and fear. And this was on the night of Sunday, twelfth
Dhul-Hijjah in the year 401 of Hijra.

THE TWENTY-SECOND DISCOURSE

He (may Allah be pleased with him) said:
It is a practice of Allah to try His believing servant in
proportion to his faith. Thus if a person's faith is great and
immense, his trial is also great. Thus the trial of a *Rasul* is
greater than that of a *Nabi*, because his faith is greater than
that of the latter. And the trial of the *Nabi* is greater than that
of a *Badal (Abdal)*. And the trial of a *Badal* is greater than that
of a *Wali*. Everyone is tried according to his faith and certainty.
And the authority for this lies in a saying of the Holy Prophet
(Allah's peace be on him): "Verily we the community of
Prophets are most tried of all people."
Then Allah keeps the trials in continuance for these
honourable leaders according to their grades, so that they may

always remain in His presence and may never slacken in their wakefulness. He the Exalted loves them and they are the people of love and the beloved of Allah and the lover never likes to be away from his beloved.

Thus the trials are restrainers of their hearts and a kind of imprisonment for their souls and keep them restrained from inclination towards anything which is not their object of life, and from feeling comfortable and inclined to anything besides their Creator. So, when this becomes their permanent feature, their desires get melted and their selves become broken and the truth becomes distinguished from falsehood, then their designs and purposes and will and inclination towards all enjoyments and comforts of this life and of the hereafter become withdrawn and contracted in a corner of their mind and the solace of their mind comes to rest in the promise of Allah and their pleasure in His decree and their contentment in His gift and their patience in His trial and they become safe from the evil of His creation; and all this to the extent of their heart's desire.

Thus will the power of the heart be strengthened and it will acquire control over all the organs of the body. Because trials and calamities strengthen the heart and certainty and establishes the faith and patience and weakens the animal self and its desires. Because when suffering comes and the believer exhibits patience and pleasure and spirit of surrender to the act of Allah and gratitude towards Him, Allah becomes pleased with him and there comes to him help and abundance and strength. Allah the Mighty and Glorious says: "If you are grateful surely I shall give you more (xiv-7)."

And when the self of man moves the heart in search of any object of desire and any enjoyment, and the heart responds to this demand for the object and this without any command from Allah and His permission, the result is forgetfulness of Allah, and polytheism and sin. Allah seizes them (the mind and the heart) with ignominy and calamities and subjection to people and injury and anxiety and pain and disease.

But the heart and the mind are affected by this suffering. But if the heart does not respond to the call of the mind in regard to its object until permission comes from Allah through *Ilham* (minor revelation) in the case of *Awliya* and clear *Wahy* (major revelation) in the case of *Rasul* an *Nabi*, and action is taken on this revelation whether it be the bestowal of a gift or its withholding, Allah rewards the mind and the heart with mercy and blessing and comfort and pleasure and light and knowledge are nearness to Himself and independence from needs. and safety from calamities. So know all this and remember it and save yourself from trial with extreme carefulness by not making haste in responding to the call of the mind and its desire but wait patiently in such cases for the permission of the Master so that you may remain safe in this world aud the hereafter.

THE TWENTY-THIRD DISCOURSE

He (may Allah be pleased with him) said:

Stick to and be contented with the little that you have with utmost effort, until the decree of fate reaches its culmination and you are lifted towards a higher and finer state, wherein you will be made to abide and kept secure from the hardships of this world's life and of the hereafter and from evil sequel and transgression. Then you will be made to rise towards what will please your eyes all the more and will be more enjoyable. And know that your portion you will not miss by your want of seeking for it, neither will that which is not your portion can be obtained by you through your greedy efforts and attempts. for it. So hold your patience and stick with satisfaction to your present condition and be contented with it. You should not take anything by yourself nor give anything by yourself unless and until you are commanded.

And do not move on your own nor rest on your own, because if you do so you will be tried by a condition worse than yours in the creation. Because by such a lapse you will be doing injustice to yourself and Allah is not unmindful of the unjust. Allah says:

"And thus do We make some of the unjust to befriend others on account of what they earned." (vi-130)

Because you are in the house of a King whose command is great, whose power is immense, whose army is huge, whose will. is in force, whose order is irresistible, whose kingdom is everlasting, whose sovereignty is abiding, whose knowledge is subtle, whose wisdom is deep, whose judgment is absolutely equitable, from whom not even an atom can be hidden either in the earth or in the heaven nor can the injustice of the unjust person can remain concealed. While you are the most unjust one and greatest offender because moved by your animal passion you have taken the initiative in your own self and in the creation of Allah and thereby indirectly you have ascribed a partner to him Allah says:

"Verily Allah will not forgive that any partner be ascribed to Him and He will forgive what is besides that to whomsoever He pleases." (iv-116)

Keep away from associating anything with Allah with utmost effort and do not go near this sin and shun it in all your movements and restful conditions during the night as well as during the day, both in moments of solitude and when you are in company. Beware of sin in all its forms in all your organs of body and in your heart. And shun sin, what appears on the surface as well as what remains hidden. And do not run away from Allah for He will overtake you. And do not dispute with Him in His decree, for then He will crush you; and do not blame Him in regard to His order, for then He will abase you; and do not remain forgetful of Him for then He will forget you and will involve you in troubles; and do not create any innovation in His house for then He will destroy you; and do not say anything in His religion prompted by your low desire, for then He will cause you to perish and will make your heart dark and will snatch away from you your faith and your spiritual knowledge and will give your devil and your animal self and your low desires and passions and people of your family and your neighbours and your friends and your associates and the rest of His creation, even the scorpions of your house and its serpents and i s Jinns and the rest of the venomous reptiles of it, — power over you, and thus He will make your life in this world dark and will prolong your punishment in the hereafter.

THE TWENTY-FOURTH DISCOURSE

He (Allah be pleased with him) said:

Keep away from disobedience to Allah, the Exalted, the Glorious with utmost effort, and cling to His Door with truth. And apply all your power and effort in obeying Him with apologies and entreaties showing your neediness in utmost submissiveness and humility, in silence and with downcast look not looking at people, nor following your animal desires, nor seeking any recompense whether of this world or of the hereafter, nor yet any promotion to higher position or honourable stations. And know it for certain that you are His servant, and that the servant and all that he possesses belongs to his master, so that he cannot claim anything as against him. Observe good manners and do not blame your master. Everything is in an appointed measure with Him. What He puts forward no one can push back and whatever He keeps back no one can push forward. And in this way Allah acquits Himself with regard to your affairs. He has given you the abode of permanence in the Hereafter and made you the master of it and will bestow on you such gifts in the Hereafter as no eye has seen, no ear has heard, and no human heart has felt. Allah says: (xxxii-17)

"So not soul knows what is in store for them of that which will refresh the eyes, a reward for what they did." i.e. a reward for their actions in this world in carrying out the injunctions, and in exhibiting patience in eschewing what is forbidden and in surrendering and making oneself completely over to Him in all that is decreed by Him and in reconciling oneself to Him in all affairs.

But as for him whom Allah has given worldly things and made him master of them and blessed him in them and conferred His favour, He has done so because the position of this man's faith is like a barren and hard land in which it is not possible for water to stay nor for trees, crops and fruits to grow. Then He cast in it various kinds of manure and similar things which cause the plants and trees to grow, and these are the world and its materials, in order to secure by these what He has grown in it of the tree of faith and plant of deeds. If, however, these things are removed from it, the ground, the plants and the trees will be dried and the fruit will drop and the whole countryside will be desolate. And Allah, the Mighty and Glorious, wants it to be populated and in a flourishing condition.

Thus the tree of faith in a rich man is weak of growth in its root and is empty of what fills the tree of your faith. O Dervish; whereas the strength of the other thing and its continuity of existence depends on the world and its various amenities that you see with its possessor and there is nothing with him more preferable to what I have described to you. May Allah give us and you power to achieve what He loves and is pleased with by His kindness. Thus the strength and the continuity of the provisions of this world what you find with him together with various blessings,—if these things are removed from him while the tree is weak, the tree will be dried up and this rich man will become an unbeliever and will join the company of hypocrites and apostates and unbelievers, O my Allah,—unless Allah sends to this rich man armies of patience and cheerful forbearance and certainty and knowledge and various kinds of spiritual enlightenment and thereby strengthen his faith. Then of course he will not mind the disappearance of wealth and blessings.

THE TWENTY-FIFTH DISCOURSE

He (may Allah be pleased with him) said:

Do not say, O penniless man! from whom the world and its people have turned their face, who is without any fame, who is hungry and thirsty, whose body is bare of clothes, whose liver is parched, who wanders about in every corner of the world, in every mosque and in every desolate place and is turned away from every door and deprived of every object and broken down and who is fed up and disappointed with all the desires and longings of his heart,—do not say that Allah has made you poor and taken away the world from you and brought about your fall and forsaken you and has become your enemy and made you distracted and has not given you any composure of mind and abased you and has not given you enough in this world and has reduced you to obscurity and has not made your name exalted among people and your brothers while He has given others plenty of His blessings so that they are passing their nights and days in that and made them superior to you and to the people of your house, whereas both of you are Muslims and believers and have your common mother in Eve and common father in Adam the best of mankind.

Well, Allah has dealt with you in this manner because your nature is pure and the moisture of the mercy of Allah is to come to you incessantly in the form of patience and cheerful surrender and certainty and reconcilement and knowledge. And the light of faith and of monotheism is to be heaped on you. Then the tree of your faith and its root and its seed will be established and it will become firm and full of foliage and will bear fruit and will be growing and spreading out branches and causing shade and shooting forth twigs. Thus every day it will be on the increase and will grow and will not need any manure to help its growth and development. The thing which Allah has allotted to you will come to you in due time whether you welcome it or are averse to it. So you should not be greedy for what will presently be yours and do not be anxious for it. And do not feel sorry for what is meant for another person and not you.

What is not in your possession, must be either of the two; (1) either it will be yours or (2) it will be another person's. Now if it be yours it will come to you and you will be drawn towards it and the meeting will take place very soon. And what is not yours, you will be turned away from it and it will turn away from you, and so there will be no meeting between you and the thing. So be occupied in the best manner with what you are after in the time present before you in obeying your Lord and do not raise your head and do not pay any heed towards what is besides Him. Allah says:

"And do not stretch your eyes after that with which We have provided different classes of them, (of) the splendour of this world's life, that We may thereby try them and the sustenance (given) by your Lord is better and more abiding." (xx-131)

So certainly Allah has forbidden you to pay attention to anything else but that on which He has maintained you and has given you your provision of obedience; and has bestowed on

you out of His allotment and provisions and favour. And He
has warned you that whatever is besides these is a trial with
which He has been trying them (others) and that your cheerful
acceptance of your portion is better for you and purer and preferable: so let this be your way and resort and stay and your
inner and outer characteristics and your objective and your
desire and longing through which you will attain every object
and reach every station and attain every good and blessing,
freshness and joy and everything nice. Allah has said:

"No soul knows what is in store for them of that which will
refresh the eyes, a reward for what they did." (xxxii-17)

So there is no deed beyond the five prescribed ways of
service and eschewing of all the sins and there is nothing greater
and more honourable and more liked by and pleasing to Allah
than what we have mentioned for you already and may Allah
give you and us the power to do what is liked by Him and is
pleasing to Him, by His favour.

THE TWENTY-SIXTH DISCOURSE

He (may Allah be pleased with him) said:

The veil and screen from your self will not be removed
unless you get out of the creation and turn the back of your
heart against them in all conditions of life and unless your
desires vanish away and then your purpose and then your
longings and you disappear from the existence of this world an d
of the hereafter and become like a vessel with a hole in it, and
nothing remains in you of purpose excepting the purpose of
your Lord and you are filled with the light of your Lord and
there remains no place and room in your heart excepting for
your Lord and you become gatekeeper of your heart and you
are given the sword of monotheism and greatness and power.
Then whatever you see approaching the gate of your heart from
the atmosphere of your mind, you will remove its head from its
shoulder, so that there remain not for yourself and your desire
and your purpose and your longing of this world and of the
hereafter anything with its head raised and neither any world
that is listened to, nor any opinion which is followed, excepting
obedience to the commandment of the Lord and standing by

Him and cheerful acceptance of His decree, rather complete
merging in His decree and allotment. Thus you become the
servant of the Lord and not the servant of the people and their
opinion.

And when this becomes a permanent feature in your life,
curtains of self-respect will be hung around your heart and
trenches of dignity will be dug round it and the power of
greatness will surround it and your heart will be guarded by the
army of truth and monotheism and, besides this, guards of truth
will be posted near it, so that people may not have any
approach to it through the devil, through your animal self,
through passion, through purpose, through vain desires and
false claims growing in the minds of people and through misguidance growing from desires.

If it is destined that people will come to you in unbroken
succession and they will be unanimous in regard to your
greatness so that they may obtain dazzling light and clear signs
and deep wisdom and see evident miracles and supernatural
happenings as a regular feature of your life and thereby increase
in their efforts to be near Allah and to be obedient to Him and
also increase in their effort for the service of their Lord even
when all these things happen, you will be made secure from all
of them and from the inclination of your human spirit towards
desire, from self-admiration and vanity and importance attendant on a large number of people coming to you and on their
being attentive to you.

Similarly, if it is destined that you shall have a wife beautiful and graceful, responsible for her own self and for her own
maintenance, you will be made secure from her evil and will
be saved from carrying her burden and that of her retainers and
relations, and she will be for you a gift of Allah, sufficient,
blessed and harmonious in temperament and clean from
insincerity and evil-mindedness and fraud and malice and breach
of trust in your absence. Thus she will be in your subjection.
Then she and her relations will make you free from the burden
of her maintenance and will ward off from you any trouble on
her account. And if it is destined that she will beget any child
for you it will be a righteous and pure descendant who will be

pleasing to your eyes. Allah says: "And We made his wife fit for him". (xxi 90)

He further says:

"O our Lord! grant us in our wives and our offspring the joy of our eyes and make us guide to those who guard against evil." (xxv 74)

Still further He says:

"And make him my lord one in whom Thou art well pleased." (xix-6)

Thus all these prayers which are in these verses will come into action and be accepted in your case, whether or not you address these prayers to Allah because as they are, they are meant for those who are worthy of them, and are favoured with these blessings and are worthy of this position and are established in this condition and to whom the favour and nearness of Allah are allotted.

Similarly, if it is destined that a certain thing of this world will come to you it will not in such a case cause you any harm. Thus what is your portion in it will exactly come to you, purified for your sake by the act of Allah and His will and the issue of order for its reaching you. So it will reach you and you will be rewarded, provided you get it in obedience to His command, on getting it; just as you will be rewarded on performing obligatory prayer and observing obligatory fast. And you will be commanded with regard to what is not your portion that you should spend it on those who deserve it from among your friends and neighbours and the deserving among the beggars on those who deserve the Zakat money according to the needs of the circumstances. And the actual state of affairs will be revealed to you and you will be able to distinguish between the deserving and the undeserving ones, and hearsay report cannot be as good as actual experience. Then you will be white and clear in your affair on which there will be no obscurity, no ambiguity, no confusion, no doubt.

Therefore take to patience, cultivate cheerful submission, pay regard to the present, take to obscurity, remain quiet. remain composed, remain silent. remain silent! Beware! Make good your escape! Make good your escape! Make haste! Make hsate!

Fear Allah! And again fear Allah! Cast down your look! Cast down your look! Turn away your eyes! Turn away your eyes! Be modest! till the destiny reaches its appointed time and you are taken by our hand and brought to the forefront.

Then will be removed from you all that you feel heavy, after which you will be made to plunge in an ocean of favours and kindness and mercy and will be clothed with the robe of light and Divine secrets and rare knowledge Divine Then you will be made near and spoken to and given gifts and made free from need and made courageous and exalted and addressed with the words: "Surely you are in Our presence today an honourable a faithful one". (xii-54)

Then guess and estimate from the condition of Hazrat Yusuf (Joseph) alaihissalam and truthful when he was addressed in these words through the tongue of the King of Egypt who was also its chief and Fir-aun (Pharoah of Egypt). Apparently it was the tongue of the King that was speaking and expressing it but in fact the speaker was Allah, who was speaking through the tongue of knowledge. To Yusuf was given the material kingdom, which was the kingdom of Egypt, as also the kingdom of spirit which was the kingdom of knowledge, spiritual and intellectual, and nearness to Allah and distinction and high position before Allah. Thus it is that Allah says:

"And thus did We give to Yusuf power in the land – he had mastery in it where he liked." (xii-56)

The land here stands for Egypt. With regard to the kingdom of spirit Allah says:

"Thus (it was) that We might turn away from him evil and indecency, surely he was one of Our sincere servants." (xii-24)

With regard to the kingdom of knowledge He says:

"This is of what my Lord has taught me: Surely I have forsaken the religion of a people who do not believe in Allah." (xii-37)

When you are thus addressed, O truthful one, you are given an ample share of great knowledge and blessed with strength and goodness and power and general saintliness and an order which affects the spiritual as well as the non-spiritual things and are vested with the power of creation, with the permission of Allah. of things in this would even before the coming of the hereafter. Then in the hereafter you will be in the abode of peace and in high paradise. And the sight of the countenance of Allah will be an additional thing and a favour and it is an objective which has no limit and no end.

THE TWENTY-SEVENTH DISCOURSE

He (Allah be pleased with him) said:

Regard good and evil as two fruits coming out from two branches of one single tree. One of the two branches yields sweet fruit and the other bitter. So you leave cities and countries and the outlying part of countries where fruits plucked from this tree are sent, and keep away from them and their people. And approach the tree itself and become its guard and attendant servant and acquire knowledge of these two branches and of the two fruits and their neighbourhoods and remain near the branch which yields sweet fruit; then it will be your food and your source of strength and beware lest you should approach the other branch and eat the fruit thereof and thus its bitterness should kill you. When you persist in this attitude you will be in ease, in security and safety from all troubles because troubles and all kinds of calamities are born of this bitter fruit. And when you are away from this tree and wander about in countries and these fruits are brought before you and they are mixed up in a manner that the sweet cannot be distinguished from the bitter and you start eating them, your hand may fall on the bitter and you may put it in your mouth and eat a part of it and chew it so that its bitterness goes to your palate and then your throat and further to your brain and nostrils and spreads its effect on you as far as your veins and the organs of your body and you are thus killed. Your throwing away the remainder from your mouth and washing off its effect cannot take away from you what has already spread in your body and will not benefit you.

And if you eat in the beginning the sweet fruit and its sweetness spreads in different parts of your body and you are benefited thereby and become happy, even this is not enough for you. It is inevitable that you will eat another fruit and you cannot be sure that this other one will not be bitter; so you will experience what I have already mentioned for you.

Thus it is no good to be far from the tree and to be ignorant of its fruit; and safety lies in being near to it and in standing by it. So good and evil are both acts of Allah the Mighty, the Glorious. "Allah has created you as well as what you do." (xxxvii-96)

And the Holy Prophet (peace and blessings of Allah be upon him) has said: "Allah has created the man who slaughters as well as the animal slaughtered."

And the actions of Allah's servant are His creation as also the fruit of that labour. Allah, the Mighty, the Glorious, has said:

"Enter the garden of paradise because of what you have been doing." (xvi-32)

Glory be to Him, how generous and merciful of Him! He ascribes the actions to them and says that their entry into paradise is on account of their deeds whereas these deeds owe their existence to His help and mercy. The Holy Prophet (peace and blessings of Allah be upon him) has said: "No one enters paradise on account of his own deeds." He was asked: "And even not you, O Prophet of Allah?" He said: "Yes, not even I, unless Allah covers me with His mercy" And while saying this He placed his hand on his head. This is narrated in one of the narrations of Hazrat Ayisha Siddiqua, (may Allah's blessings be upon her), (Allah be pleased with her). Thus when you are obedient to Allah in carrying out His behests and refraining from what He has forbidden, be resigned to Him in what He has appointed; He will protect you from His evil and increase His good for you and will protect you from all evils, religious and worldly. As for worldly things there is a word of Allah:

"Thus (it was) that We might turn away from him evil and indecency; surely he was one of Our sincere servants." (xxiv-12), (xii-24)

And as for religion He says:

"Why should Allah chastise you if you are grateful and believer?" (iv-147)

Indeed what will a calamity do to a person who is a believer and grateful? Because he is nearer to safety than to calamity inasmuch as he is in a state of plenty because of his gratefulness. Allah says:

"If you are grateful, surely We shall multiply (Our favours) on you." (xiv-7).

Thus your faith will quench the fire in the hereafter—the fire which will be the punishment of every sinner. How can it be then that it will not quench the fire of calamity in this life, O my Allah? Unless it be some servant in a state of spiritual ecstasy and has been selected for *wilayat* and for Divine choice. In such a case calamities are inevitable but these are to make him free from the abomination of passions and low inclination of nature and from relying upon the desires of the flesh and its enjoyments and from being contented with people and from the pleasure felt in their nearness and from living with them and from feeling pleased with them. So he is tried until all these weaknesses depart from him and his heart is purified by the expulsion of the whole lot of them, so that what remains in it is unity of the Lord and knowledge of truth and it becomes the landing place of many kinds of secrets from the unseen and knowledge and light of nearness. This is because it is a house in which there is no room for two. As Allah says:

"Allah has not made for any man two hearts within him." (xxxiii-5)

Again:

"Surely the kings, when they enter a town, ruin it and make the noblest of its people to be low." (xxvii-34).

Then they turn out the nobles from their good positions and comfortable life. And the sovereignty over the heart was (in the beginning) of the devil of desires, and selfishness. And the organs and the faculties used to be moved by their order for various sins, vanities and trifles. This sovereignty now vanishes and the organs become restful, and the house of the king becomes clear, and the courtyard, which is the breast, becomes clean. Now the heart has become clean and has become the habitation of the unity of Allah and of knowledge, and as for the courtyard it has become the alighting ground of wonderful things from the unseen. All this is the result of calamities and trial and their fruit. The Holy Prophet (peace and blessings of Allah be upon him) has said:

"We Prophets are beset with the greatest number of trials among people, then others and still others according to rank."

He has also said:

"I know more of Allah than any of you, and am more afraid of Him than any of you."

Anyone who is near the king must have his danger and guardedness of necessity increased because he is in the presence of the King from whose observation nothing is now hidden of his manipulations and movements.

Now if you say that the whole creation in the sight of Allah is like one man, that nothing of it remains hidden from Him, what then is the good of this statement? You are to be told that when a person's position is raised and he is placed in an honourable rank, risks also become great, because it has become necessary for him to give thanks for what He has conferred on him, in the shape of various blessings and favours. So that slightest diversion from service to Him is a default in gratitude to Him and is a shortcoming in one's obedience to Him. Thus Allah says:

"O wives of the Prophet! whosoever of you commits an open indecency, the chastisement shall be increased to her doubly." (xxxiii-30).

Allah says so to these ladies on account of His having completed His blessings on them by bringing them in contact with the Holy Prophet (may Allah's peace and blessings be upon him). What will then be the position of one who is attached to Allah and is near Him ? Allah is far too high and above all similitude with His creation.

"Nothing is like unto a likeness of Him and He is the Hearing and the Seeing." (xlii-11).

THE TWENTY-EIGHTH DISCOURSE

He (may Allah be pleased with him) said:

So you wish for comfort and joy and happiness and safety and peace, to be blessed and carefree, while you are still in the crucible and in the course of killing your animal self and are in the midst of a struggle with your desires and that of removing your objects and with the hope for returns in this world and in the hereafter and the remnant of these still remains with you in a very potent form? On hasty one! halt and walk slowly; O you expectant! the door is closed, still this state continues. And surely some remnants of these things are still on you and some small particles of it are still in you. It is an emancipation contract of a slave; so long as even a penny is left on it, you are shut out from it. So long as there remains with you the measure of sucking the stone of a date from this world and from your desires and purpose and longing and from your seeing anything of this world or seeking anything or liking anything from the returns of this world or the hereafter—so long as anything among these things persists in you, you are still at the door of self-annihilation. You stop here until you acquire the annihilation completely and perfectly and then you are taken out of the crucible and your seasoning is complete and you are adorned with ornaments and dressed and perfumed and incensed, then you are taken to the great King and addressed with the words :

"Surely you are in Our presence an honourable and faithful one." (xii-54).

Then you will be provided with comforts and shown gentleness and fed with His favour and also given drink and will be made near and will be enlightened on secrets, which will not be hidden from you. And you will be made free from want on account of what you will be given out of these things, free from the need of all things. Do you not see the pieces of gold, of various shapes, changing and circulating morning and evening, in the hands of druggists and green-grocers and butchers and tanners and oilmen and sweepers and people of various crafts both very fine and lowly and dirty? Then these pieces are collected together and placed in the crucible of the goldsmith; then they melt with the flames of fire, then they are taken out of the crucible and pounded and softened and seasoned to make them into ornaments and polished and perfumed and then left unto best places and houses, behind locks, in treasuries and boxes and dark places or they are made to adorn the body of a bridge

and they are ornamented and given honour, and sometimes
the bridge may be of a great king. Thus the pieces of gold pass
from the hands of tanners to the presence of kings and to the
court after being melted and pounded. In this way you, O believer, if you show patience on the enforcement of the allotment
of Providence and give cheerful submission to His decree, in
every condition of life, you will be made near to your Lord in
this world and you will be blessed with knowledge of Him and
other kinds of knowledge and secrets and will be given residence
in the hereafter in the abode of peace with the Prophets and
the *Saddiqs* and the *Shahids* and the *Salihs* in the proximity
of Allah and in His house and near Him enjoying His kindness.
So show patience and do not make haste and remain pleased
with the decree of Providence and do not complain against Him.
If you do so you will get the coolness of His forgiveness and
the sweetness of knowledge about Him and His kindness and
favour.

THE TWENTY-NINTH DISCOURSE

He (may Allah be pleased with him) said :

On the saying of the Holy Prophet (may peace and blessings
of Allah be upon him) : "Poverty may . well nigh lead to
unbelief."

The servant believes in Allah and surrenders all his affairs to
Allah; has his faith in the easy providence of sustenance from
Him and has also the firm conviction that whatever is to come
to him can by no means miss him and that whatever misses him
can by no means come to him and that :

"Whoever is dutiful towards Allah He makes a way out for
him and gives him sustenance from where he cannot expect and
whoever relies on Allah He is sufficient for him." (lxv-2, 3).

He says all this while he is in a state of ease and comfort;
then Allah tries him with calamity and poverty; so he takes to
position and humble entreaty; but He does not remove these
things from him. It is then that the truth of the Holy Prophet's
(may peace and blessings be upon him) saying: "Poverty may
well nigh lead to unbelief," becomes established. Then as for
him with whom Allah deals gently, He removes from him what

afflicts him and gives him comfort and affluence and gives him power to be thankful and to give praise to Allah and He continues doing so till the man meets Him. And when Allah wants to try him, He perpetuates His calamity and poverty and cuts off from him the help of faith. Then he shows unbelief by finding fault with and accusing Allah and by doubting in His promise. So he dies an unbeliever in Allah disputing His signs and feeling angry at his Lord. It is to such a man that the Holy Prophet of Allah (peace and blessings of Allah be upon him) refers in his saying :

"Verily the man who is most severely punished of all people on the Day of Resurrection is one to whom Allah has given both poverty in this life and chastisement in the hereafter." We ask the protection of Allah from such a plight."

And the poverty spoken of in the saying is the one that makes man forgetful of Allah and it is from this that he has sought His protection. And the other man whom Allah wants to choose and select and whom He has included among His favourites and friends and successors of His Prophets and has marked out as a chief of His *Walis* and a great man among His servants and their learned men and their intercessors and their guides towards their Master and their instructors in the path of guidance and in avoiding the evil ways—to such a man He sends mountains of patience and oceans of the spirit of cheerful submission and reconcilement, and of total merging in the act of Allah. Then He confers on him plenty of His gifts and nurtures him with lavish care during all hours of night and day, in company as well as in solitude, sometimes in open, sometimes in secret; in the latter cash with various kinds of kindness and affection; and these things he continues to get till the moment of his death.

THE THIRTIETH DISCOURSE

He (may Allah be pleased with him) said :

How often you say, What shall I do and what means shall I adopt (for the attainment of my objective)? So you are told— stay at your own place and do not go beyond your limit till a way out comes to you from Him who has commanded you to stay where you are. Allah says :

"O you who believe, be patient and excel in patience and remain steadfast and be careful of your duty to Allah." (iii-200)

He has commanded you to be patient, O believer, then to vie one another in patience and to be steadfast and to remain on guard and to make this incumbent on yourself. He further warns you against discarding patience as in the words, "Be careful of your duty to Allah," and this is in respect of discarding this virtue. And this means that you should not give up patience. Thus good and safety lies in patience. And the Holy Prophet (peace and blessings of Allah be upon him) has said :

"Patience stands in the same relation to faith as head stands in relation to the bod·· "

And it is also said that for everything there is a reward according to a measure but for the reward of patience it will be a price which has no measure. As Allah says :

"Verily the patient will be given their reward without any measure." (xxxix-10)

So when you have been careful about your duty to Him in virtue of patience and in paying full regard to the limits set by Allah, He will reward you as He has promised you in His book:

"And whoever is careful of his duty to Allah He will make for him an outlet, and give him sustenance from whence he thinks not." (lxv-123)

And remain in your patience with those who trust in Allah till the way out comes to you because Allah has promised you sufficiency in His words :

"And whoever trusts in Allah, He is sufficient for him." (lxv-3)

And stick to patience and to trust in Allah in the company of those who do good to others as surely Allah has promised you rewards for this, as He says :

"And thus do We reward those who do good to others." (vi-85)

And Allah will love you on account of this virtue, because He has said : "Surely Allah loves the doers of good to others". (iii-133)

Thus patience is the source of all virtues and all kinds of safety in this world and in the hereafter and through it the

believer rises to the state of cheerful surrender and reconcilement to the will of Allah and then attains the state of merging
in the acts of Allah which is the state of *Badaliyyat* or *Ghaibat*.
So beware that you do not miss it so that you may not be
abased in this world and in the hereafter and the prosperity of
both these passes away from you.

THE THIRTY-FIRST DISCOURSE

He (may Allah be pleased with him) said
When you find in your heart any hatred or love for a person,
examine his actions in the light of the Book of Allah and the
practice of the Holy Prophet (may Allah's peace and blessings
be upon him). Then if they are hateful in the eyes of these two
authorities, be happy to be in accord with Allah and His Prophet (may Allah's peace and blessings be upon him). And if
his actions happen to be pleasing to them and you are inimical
to him, then know that surely you are a follower of your low
desire. You are hating him on account of your low desire,
being unjust to him on account of your hatred for him and
rebelling against Allah, the Mighty, the Glorious, and against His
Holy Prophet (may Allah's peace and blessings be upon him) and
opposing both these authorities. So turn towards Allah, repent-
ing for your hatred and ask from Him love for that man and
for others from among the friends of Allah and His *Walis* and
His selected ones and from among the pious men among His
servants and you should be in harmony with Allah in loving
him.

And you should act in the same way in the case of one
whom you love. That is to say, you should examine his actions
in the light of the Book of Allah and the practice of His Holy
Prophet (may Allah's peace and blessings be upon him). Then
if he happens to be dear to these two authorities you should
love him. But if they are hateful to him, you should hate him,
so that you may not love him through your low desire and hate
him through your low desire. Surely you are commanded to
oppose your low desire, Allah says :

"And do not follow the low desire, so that it may not lead
you astray from the path of Allah" (xxxviii-26)

THE THIRTY-SECOND DISCOURSE

He (may Allah be pleased with him) said :

How often do you say, "Whomsoever I love, my love for him does not endure. Separation intervenes between us, either through absence or through death or through enmity or through the destruction or loss of wealth." So you are told – do you not know, O believer in Allah, on whom Allah has conferred gifts, the one whom Allah has paid attention to, one whom Allah guards with jealous care, do you not know that surely Allah is jealous. He has created you for Himself and you are desirous of belonging to somebody else than Him. Have you not heard His words : "He loves them, and they love Him" (v. 54) ? As also His commandment

"And I have not created the Jinn and the men, but that they should serve me." (li-56).

Or have you not heard the saying of the Holy Prophet (may Allah's peace and blessings be upon them) : "When Allah loves a servant He puts him in a trial ; then if he shows patience, He looks after him." He was asked : "O Prophet of God (may peace and blessings of Allah be upon him), and what is His looking after ? He said : "He does not leave for him any wealth or any children."

And this is because when he has any wealth or children whom he loves, his love for his Lord becomes divided, then it becomes diminished and scattered, then it is distributed between Allah and others and Allah does not brook any partner and He is jealous and He is powerful over all things and predominant over all. So He destroys His partner and annihilates it in order to monopolise the heart of His servant for His ownself to the exclusion of all others. Then will be proved the truth of the word of Allah: "He will love them and they will love him." (v-54)

Till at last the heart becomes clear of all partners of Allah and idols such as wife and wealth and children and enjoyments and fashions and longing for dominions and kingdoms, for miracles and spiritual states and spiritual stages and stations and gardens of heaven and spiritual grades and nearness to Allah—

no purpose will remain in the heart and no desire. Then the heart
will become like a vessel with a hole in which no liquid can stay,
because it is now broken by the act of Allah. Whenever any
purpose grows therein, the act of Allah and His jealousy break
it. Then screens of dignity and might and awe are hung round
it and besides this trenches of greatness and might are dug.

Thus no desire about anything will be able to approach the
heart. Then nothing of wealth and children and wife and
friends and miracles and authority and power of interpretation
will be able to do any harm to the heart. Then surely all these
things will remain outside the heart, and therefore they will not
excite the jealousy of Allah. Rather all these things will be a sign
of honour from Allah for His servant and His kindness towards
him and His blessings and sustenance and a thing beneficial to
those who go to Him. Thus these people are honoured by this
and shown mercy thereby and protected through this investment
of honour from Allah who will be their guard and police and
shelter and intercessor in this life and in the hereafter.

THE THIRTY-THIRD DISCOURSE

He (may Allah be pleased with him) said:

There are four kinds of men. One is who has no tongue and
no heart and he is a man of ordinary position, dull and lowly,
who does not count with Allah and one who has nothing good
in him. He and people like him are like chaff which has no
weight, unless Allah covers them with His mercy and guides
their heart towards faith in Himself and moves the organs of
their body in obedience to Himself. Beware that we do not
become one of them and do not entertain them nor mind them
nor yet stand among them. These are the people of chastisement
and wrath and anger of Allah; they are the inhabitants of fire
and its inmates. We seek the refuge of Allah from them. You
should on the contrary be equipped with Divine knowledge
and be among the teachers of good and guides for religion and
its leaders and inviters thereto. So beware that you should
come to them and invite them to obedience to Allah and warn
them against sinning against Allah. Thus you will be a fighter
in the cause of Allah and will be given the rewards of prophets

and messengers of Allah. The Holy Prophet (may peace and blessings of Allah be upon him) said Hazrat Ali Karramallahu Wajbu :

"If Allah gives guidance to one person through your guiding him, it is better for you than that on which the sun rises."

The other kind of person has got a tongue but no heart; he speaks on wisdom but does not act according to it. He calls people to Allah but himself flees from Him. He abhors defects in others but he himself persists in a similar defect in himself. He shows to others his piety but contends with Allah by committing major sins. And when he is alone he is like a wolf in sheep's clothing. Here is a person against whom the Holy Prophet (may Allah's peace and blessings be upon him) has warned. He has said

"The thing to be most afraid of and which I am afraid of in respect of my followers is the evil learned men."

We seek the refuge of Allah from such learned men. So you should keep away from such a man and run away from him, lest you should be carried away by the sweetness of his talk and then the fire of his sin will burn you and the filth of his inside and heart should kill you.

There is a third kind of man who has a heart but no tongue and he is a believer. Allah had screened him away from His creation and hung round him His curtains and given him an insight into the blemishes of his own self and enlightened his heart and made him aware of the mischiefs of mixing with people and of the evil of talking and speaking and who has become sure that safety is in silence and retirement in a corner, as the Holy Prophet (peace and blessings of Allah be upon him) has said : "Whoever kept silent attained salvation." And as further he has said : "Surely the service of Allah consists of ten parts, nine of which are in silence." Thus this man is a friend of Allah in His secrets, protected, possessing safety and plenty of intelligence, companion of the Beneficent Allah, blessed with His favours and as for good, everything good is with him. So mind, you must keep company with such a man and mix with him and render him service and endear yourself to him by fulfilling the needs which he may feel, and providing him with things which will give ease and comfort. If you do these things Allah will love you and choose you and include you in the company of His friends and pious servants together with His blessings, if it pleases Him.

The fourth kind of man is one who is invited to the world invisible, clothed in dignity, as it is related in the tradition :

"Whoever learns and acts upon his learning and imparts it to others is invited to the world invisible and made great."

Such a man is possessed of the knowledge of Allah and His sign and his heart is made the repository of the rare things of His knowledge and He intimates to him such secrets as He has kept hidden from others and He has selected him and drawn him towards Himself and guided him and raised him towards Himself and expanded his heart for the acceptance of these secrets and points of knowledge and made him a worker in His cause and inviter of Allah's servants to the path of virtue and warner against the chastisement of evil deeds and an argument of Allah in their midst, a guide and a rightly-guided man, an intercessor and one whose intercession has been accepted, a truthful man and one who verifies the truth of other, a deputy of Allah's prophets and messengers, on whom be the blessings of Allah.

So this man is the end and culminating point of mankind and there is no station above this, excepting that of prophethood. So it is your duty to beware that you do not oppose such a man and be averse to him and keep away from him and be hostile to him and avoid accepting him and being attentive towards what he says and admonishes. So verily safety lies in what such a man says and also in his company, and destruction and misguidance in what is besides him; except such men whom Allah gives power and assistance towards truth and mercy.

So I have divided mankind for you (into four divisions). Now you have to look at your ownself if you have an observant mind and save yourself in the light of it if you are anxious to save it, having love for it. May Allah guide us and you towards what He loves and is pleased with, in this world and the hereafter! Ameen.

THE THIRTY-FOURTH DISCOURSE

He (may Allah be pleased with him) said

How strange that you should be angry with your Lord and blame Him and find fault with Him and ascribe to Him, the Mighty, the Glorious, injustice and delay in the matter of allotting sustenance and sufficiency and in the removal of calamities. Do you not know that for every course of events there is an appointed time and for every calamity there is a point of consummation? Neither can it be made earlier nor deferred. And the times of calamities do not change so as to give place to comfort and the time of difficulty does not change into that of affluence. Adopt the best of manners and stick to silence and patience and cheerful submission and reconcilement with your Lord and repent for your angry attitude towards Allah and your accusations of Him in the matter of His action.

In the presence of Allah there is no room for demanding one's due in full nor for retaliation without incurring any sin, in response, to the urge of nature, such as is to be found in the case of mutual relationship between His servants. He, the Mighty and the Glorious, is absolutely alone, from eternity existing before, everything and He created the things and created their benefits and harms. So He knows their beginning and their end and their ultimate object and their sequel. And He, the Mighty and the Glorious, is wise in the matter of His action and is firm in His fashioning of things and there is no contradiction in His acts. And He does not do anything without any meaning and does not create anything without any purpose and in a playful manner. And it is not proper that any defect or blame should be ascribed to His deeds. You should rather wait for relief if you feel exhausted in your reconcilement with Him and in exhibiting a spirit of cheerful submission and of merging in His action, till the time of the decree of providence reaches its appointed time and the trying conditions change into their opposite by the passage of time and the consummation of the course of events, in the same way as the winter attains its consummation and makes room for summer and the night attains consummation and makes room for the day.

Thus if you ask for the light of day during the increasing darkness of the evening it will not be given you ; rather the darkness of the night will increase till when the darkness reaches its end and the time of dawn approaches, the day comes with its light whether you ask and desire for it or keep silence over it and dislike it. So if you want the return of the night at that time your prayer will not be granted because you have asked for a thing untimely. So you will be left to lament and deprived and disgusted and ashamed. So leave all this and stick to reconcilement and good faith with your Lord and graceful patience. So what is yours will not be snatched away from you and what is not yours will not be given to you. By my faith it is so, provided that you ask from Allah and seek His help by prayer and entreaty, worshipping Him and obeying Him and carrying out His orders in pursuance of His commandment : "Call on me and I will accept your prayers." (xl-60). And of His another commandment : "Apply to Allah for His favour." (iv-32). And of similar other verses of the Quran and sayings of the Holy Prophet (may Allah's peace and blessings be upon him). And you will pray to Him and He will accept your prayer in its appointed time and at the end of its appointed term and when He wills, and also if there is any advantage for you in this, in your worldly life and in the world hereafter or the same accords with His dispensation and with the end of the fixed term.

Do not blame Him when He delays the acceptance of your prayer and do not get exhausted in your prayer, for verily if you do not gain you do not lose anything either. If He does not accept your prayer immediately in this world's life. He will give you a deferred reward in the life to come. There is a tradition handed down from the Holy Prophet (may Allah's peace and blessings be upon him) which purports to say that on the Day of Resurrection the servant of Allah will find in His book of deeds some good deeds which he will not recognise ; then he will be told that these are in exchange for his prayers in his worldly life that were not destined to be accepted or something to that effect as it is narrated in the tradition. So the least of your spiritual state should be that you should be remembering your Lord adhering strictly to your faith in His

unity while asking anything from Him and that you should not
ask from anybody else and not carry your need to anybody
excepting Him. So at all times, during night or day, in health
or illness, in adversity or prosperity, in difficulty or ease, you
are in either of the two conditions :

(1) Either you refrain from asking and remain satisfied and
reconciled and surrendered to His act like a dead body before
one who gives it the funeral bath or like a sucking baby in the
hand of a nurse or like a polo-ball before the polo-rider,
who makes it turn and revolve with his polo stick. Thus
does Providence turn as it likes. If it happens to be a
blessing, thanks and praise go forth from you, and an increase
comes from Him, the Mighty, the Glorious, in the gift, as He
said :

"Verily if you are grateful, most surely, I will give to you
more." (xiv-7)

But if it be an adversity, patience and reconcilement goes
forth from you with the help of the strength given by Him, and
firmness of heart and help and blessing and mercy from Him,
as He the Mighty, the Glorious, says: "Surely Allah is with the
Patient" (ii-153). That is to say, He is with the patient with
His favours such as help and strength ; and as He says :

"If you help Allah, He will help you and make firm your
feet". (xlvii-7)

When you have helped (the cause of) Allah, by opposing
your low desires and by giving up finding fault with Him and
refraining from being displeased with His action with regard
to yourself and you become an enemy to your ownself for
the sake of Allah, ready to strike it with the sword whenever
it moves with its unbelief and ploytheism, and you cut
off its head with your patience and reconcilement to your
Lord, as also with your satisfaction with His act and promise
and pleasure with both of them, – if you do so, Allah will
be your Helper. And as for blessing and mercy there is His
word :

"And give good news to the patient, those when a misfortune befalls them, they say : Surely we are Allah's and to Him
we shall return. Those are they on whom are blessings and

mercy from their Lord, and those are the followers of the right course. (ii-156-157)

(2) And the other alternative condition is that you supplicate before Allah with prayer, and humble entreaties, regarding Him as great, and being obedient to His orders. Yes, do call on Allah and it is keeping a thing in its proper place, because He Himself urges you to ask from Him and turn towards Him and has made it a means to your comfort, and a kind of messenger from you to Him, and a medium of contact with Him and a means of access to Him, provided, of course, that you refrain from putting any blame on Him and from being angry with Him, in the event of the acceptance of your prayer being deferred to its appointed time. So, take note of the difference between the two conditions and do not go beyond the bounds of both, because there is no other condition besides these. So beware lest you should be among the unjust ones, who transgress the limits. In that cause He will destroy you and He will not care, as He destroyed those people who have gone before in this world by intensifying His calamities, and in the next life by a painful chastisement. Glory, be to Allah, the Great! O the Knower of my condition! on You is my reliance.

THE THIRTY-FIFTH DICOURSE

He (may Allah be pleased with him) said:

Abstinence from unlawful things is incumbent on you or else the rope of destruction is coiled round you. You can never get out of its tangle unless Allah covers you with His mercy. There is an authentic report from the Holy Prophet (peace and blessings of Allah be upon him) that the foundation of religion is abstinence from unlawful things and its destruction is in greed, and that whoever goes round a protected pasture-land is only too likely to help himself to it as a cattle pasturing freely by the side of a cornfield is only too likely to stretch his mouth towards it. It is unlikely that the cornfield should remain safe from him. Hazrat Umar Ibn Khattab (may Allah be pleased with him) is reported to have said:

"We used to abstain from nine-tenth of lawful things in the fear lest we should fall in the zone of unlawful things."

And it is reported from Hazrat Abu Bakr Siddiq (may Allah be pleased with him) that he said:

"We used to avoid seventy doors of permissible things for fear of getting involved in sin."

These personages did so just to be away from any proximity to unlawful things; and in doing so they acted on the saying of the Holy Prophet (peace and blessings of Allah be upon him):

"Beware! verily every king has a protected pasture-land and the pasture-land of Allah is His forbidden things."

Thus whoever goes round the pasture-land is likely to get into it; but one who enters the fort of the king and passes through the first, then the second and then the third gate till he approaches the threshold, is better than one who stands at the first door which is contiguous to the open country side. So if the third door is shut against him it will not harm him as he is still behind two doors of the palace and has the treasury of the king and his army near him. But as for the man who is at the first gate, if this one is closed upon him, he remains alone in the open land and he may be seized by wolves and enemies and may be among the destroyed ones. Similarly, one who treads the path of Allah's appointed duties and makes it incumbent upon himself, the help of power and concession is taken away from him and he is cut off from these, he will still be on leave ; and he will not be outside the law. So when death overtakes him he will be found on obedience and service and his good work will be borne testimony to.

And one who stands on leave and permission and does not advance towards the obligatory duties, if the resource is snatched away and he is cut off from His help, low desire and passions of the animal self will overpower him, he will indulge in unlawful things and get out of the law and join the company of devils who are the enemies of Allah and shall have gone astray from the right path. So if death overtakes him before repentance he will be among the perished ones unless Allah covers him with His mercy and favours. So every danger lies in standing on leave and permission and every safety in standing on obligatory duties.

THE THIRTY-SIXTH DISCOURSE

He (may Allah be pleased with him) said :

Make your life after death your capital and your worldly life—its profit. Spend your time first of all in acquiring your life after death. Then if any surplus time is left spend it in acquiring your worldly life, in seeking your livelihood. And do not make your worldly life your capital and your life after death your profits, so as to spend any surplus time left in obtaining your life after death and to fulfil the obligations of five prayers in that, as if putting all together in a single melting pot, dropping its different parts and upsetting the order of various obligations, without the ritual bending and prostration and without restful pause between different parts; or when you are exhausted and agitated you take to sleep, leaving the whole thing unattended, like a dead body during the night and whiling away the day in obedience to your animal self and your animal desire and your devil and selling your hereafter in exchange for your worldly life, acting like a slave of the animal self and its riding beast. You are commanded to ride on your animal self and to discipline it and to exercise it and to traverse on its back the paths of safety, that is the way to the life eternal and to the obedience to its Lord. But you have acted unjustly towards it by accepting its urges and you have handed over to it its reins and followed it in its low desires and in its enjoyments, and you have made an alliance with its devil and its passion, so you have missed the best thing of this life and of the hereafter and have incurred loss in respect of both of them, and thus you enter on the Day of Judgment the poorest of men and the greatest loser in respect of religion, and without obtaining, by following it, most of your allotted portion in this world's life. On the other hand, if you had traversed with it the path of the hereafter and used it as your capital you would have gained in your worldly life as well as in the hereafter; and your destined portion of this world's life would have come to you with all its pleasantness and you would have been secure and respected. Thus the Holy Prophet may Allah's peace and blessings be upon him has said:

"Surely Allay gives felicity in this world's life on the intention pertaining to the hereafter, whereas the felicity of the hereafter is not given on the intention pertaining to this world's life."

And how can it be otherwise? And the intention for the hereafter is the obedience to Allah because the intention is the very soul of service and its very being. So when you obey Allah with your abstinence in this world's life and with seeking the abode of the hereafter you become among the chosen ones of Allah and the people of obedience to and love for Him and the life hereafter is obtained by you and that is the paradise and nearness to Allah. And the world will be at your service and the portion allotted to you from it will be given to you in full, because everything is subordinate to its Creator and its Master. And if you get engrossed in the worldly life and turn your face from the hereafter, the Lord will be angry with you; you will lose the hereafter and the world will be disobedient to you and will put you in trouble and difficulty in the matter of allowing your allotted portion to reach you, on account of the anger of Allah towards you because it is owned by Allah; so it abases whoever is disobedient to Him. Then it is that the truth of a saying of the Holy Prophet may Allah's peace and blessings be upon him is established and the saying is this:

"The world and the hereafter are two co-wives; if you please any of the two the other becomes angry with you."

Allah, the Mighty, the Glorious, says:

"Surely there are among you who desire this world's life and some others among you who desire the hereafter." (ii-151).

These are called the children of the world and the children of the hereafter respectively. Then see which of these two you are children of and to which of these two tribes you like to belong while you are in this world. Then when you pass on to the other life there will be one party in the heaven and the other party in the hell. Then one section of people shall remain standing at their own place in the midst of prolonged reckoning on a day which, as the word of Allah says, is the equivalent of fifteen thousand years. Then there will be another section of people that shall be staying by the dining table on which will be very good food and fruits and honey whiter than ice, as it has been narrated in the Hadith:

"They shall be looking at their residence in Heaven, until when Allah will be free from the account of the people, they will enter the heaven: they shall find their way towards their residences just as a man in this world finds his way to his residence."

Evidently these people attain to this position only by their discarding the world and by their occupying themselves with and their attempt to get the hereafter and the Master; and those other people are involved in the accounts and various kinds of difficulties and humiliations only on account of their preoccupations with the world and their attachment to it and their indifference towards the hereafter and the scantiness of their attention towards its affairs and their forgetfulness of the Day of Judgment and what is to happen to them in the future among the things mentioned in the Book of Allah and the Traditions of the Holy Prophet may Allah's peace and blessings be upon him. So look at your own self with the look of mercy and affection and choose for it the one that is better among the two groups and keep it away from bad associates and from the disobedient from among men and Jinns and make the Book of Allah and the *Sunnah* your guide and look at these two authorities with contemplation and meditation and act on them and do not be deceived by mere talk, and by greed. Allah says:

"What the Prophet has brought to you accept it and what he has forbidden you refrain from it and be careful of your duty to Allah (lix-7).

And do not oppose him so that you may not cease acting on what he has brought. Do not make innovation from your own self either with regard to deeds or with regard to service, as Allah says in respect of a people who went away from the right path:

"And as for monasticism they innovated it; We did not prescribe it to them." (lvii-27).

Accordingly He purified His Prophet and kept him away from falsehood. Thus He says:

"Nor does he speak out of desire. It is naught but revelation which is revealed." (liii-34).

Meaning: "Whatever has been brought to you it is from Me and not from his desire and self, so follow it."

He further says:

"If you love Allah then follow me, Allah will love you." (iii-31).

So it is clear that the path of love is to follow him in word and deed. Thus the Holy Prophet (peace and blessings of Allah be upon him) says: "Earning is my way and reliance on Allah is my state."

So you are between his practice and his state. If your faith is weak you should take to earning which is his practice and if your faith is strong you adopt your state which is reliance on Allah. Allah the Mighty, the Glorious, says: "And on Allah you should rely." And He also says:

"And whoever trusts in Allah He is sufficient for him." (lxv-3).

He further says:

"Surely Allah loves those who trust in Him." (iii-158).

So He commands you to have trust in Him and insists on your sticking to it just as His Prophet has been commanded to observe the same. And the Holy Prophet (peace and blessings of Allah be upon him) says:

"Whoever does a deed on which there is no commandment of ours is rejected".

This covers livelihood and deeds and words. We have no Prophet excepting him whom we can follow, and no book excepting the Quran on which we can act. So do not go beyond these two, lest you should perish and lest your desires and the devil should lead you astray:

"Do not follow desire so that it will lead you astray from the path of Allah." (xxxviii-26).

And safety lies in the Bcok of Allah and the practice of the Holy Prophet may Allah's peace and blessings be upon him and destruction in what is besides them and with the help of these two the servant of Allah rises towards the state of *Wilayat,* of *Badaliyyat* and of *Ghauthiyyat.*

THE THIRTY-SEVENTH DISCOURSE

He (may Allah be pleased with him) said:

Why is it that I see you, O believer, envying your neighbour for his food and drink and dress and wife, and his house of residence and for his enjoying himself on his affluence, finding him in possession of blessings of his Master and of the portion allotted to him? Do you not know that it weakens your faith and causes you to fall in the eye of your Master and makes you loathsome to Him? Have you not heard the saying narrated from the Holy Prophet that Allah says: "An envious person is an enemy of Our blessing"?

And have you not heard the saying of the Holy Prophet may Allah's peace and blessings be upon him. "Verily envy eats up the virtues as fire eats up the fuel"?

Then why are you envious of him, O poor man ? Is it for his portion or for yours ? Then if you envy him for the portion allotted to him by Allah, you come under the operation of His word :

"We distribute among them their livelihood in the life of this world." (xliii. 32).

You have most surely been unjust to this man who is enjoying the blessing of his Lord with which He has specially favoured him and which He has appointed as his portion and has not left any share in it for anyone else. Then who will be more unjust than yourself and the more miserly and more foolish and stupid ? And if you envy him on account of your portion, then you have betrayed utmost of ignorance, because your portion will not be given to anybody else and will not be transferred from you to anybody else. Allah is free from such injustice. Allah says:

"The word which is with Us cannot be changed and We are not unjust to Our servants." (1-29).

Surely Allah has not been unjust to say so as to take from you what He has allotted to you and to give to somebody else. Such a thought only betrays your ignorance and is an injustice to your brother. Then it is better for you that you should be envious of the earth which is a storehouse of treasures and buried wealth, consisting of various kinds of gold, silver and

precious stones out of what had been hoarded by past kings;
of A'ad and Thamud and kings and emperors of Persia and
Rome—than that you should envy your brother.

And your likeness is only like that of a man who sees a king
with his majesty and army and power and kingdom, exercising
control over the lands and collecting their taxes and exploiting
them for his own benefit and enjoying life with various kinds of
enjoyments and gratification of desires, but he does not envy
this king, while he sees a wild dog which serves a dog from
among the dogs of that king and remains with it and passes
day and night with it and is given the leavings and crumbs of
food from the royal kitchen, so he lives on that : this man
begins envying this dog, and becomes hostile to him and desires
his death and wants meanly to be in its place after its death
without being indifferent towards the world or developing a
religious attitude towards life and contentment with his own lot.
Is there any man in the whole course of time more foolish than
this man and more stupid and more ignorant ?

Then had you known, O poor man ! what your neighbour
will have to face in the future in the form of a lengthy account
on the Day of Resurrection if he has not obeyed Allah in what
He has given him out of His blessings and in the matter of
fulfilling the obligations due to Him and if he has not obeyed
His orders and observed His prohibitions while enjoying His
blessings and has not used them as an aid to His service and
obedience to Him, he will face such things as will make him
desire that he was not given even a particle of these enjoyments.
and had never seen any enjoyment at all. Have you not heard
what has come down in the tradition

"Surely there will be parties of people who will desire on the
Day of Resurrection that their flesh might be severed from their
body by means of scissors on their seeing the recompense of the
sufferers of troubles."

So your neighbour will desire on the Day of Judgment to
be in your place in this world's life, on seeing his own lengthy
account and his own difficulties and his standing fifty thousand
years in the heat of the sun of that day on account of what he
has enjoyed of the comfort of this world's life, while you will

be keeping aside from all this under the shade of the throne of Allah, eating, drinking, enjoying, happy and joyful and comfortably placed on account of your patience in the face of difficulties of the world's life and lack of means and its troubles and its poverty and its neediness and on account of your contentment with your lot and your reconcilement to your Lord in what He has decreed and ordered in the matter of your poverty and of the affluence of others and of your ill·health and others' healthiness and of your difficulties and others' ease and comfort and of your abasement and others' honour. May Allah gather you among those who show patience in face of calamities and feel grateful for His blessings and who resign and entrust their affairs to the Lord of the earth and heaven.

THE THIRTY-EIGHTH DISCOURSE

He (may Allah be pleased with him) said :
Whoever executes the work of his Lord with sincerity and earnestness, dreads whatever is besides Him day and night. O people, do not claim what you do not possess. And proclaim the unity of Allah and do not associate anything with him and make yourself the target of the arrows of providence which will strike you not to kill but to injure, and however perishes for the sake of Allah receives his compensation from Him.

THE THIRTY-NINTH DISCOURSE

He (may Allah be pleased with him) said :
To take anything on the basis of desire without any order from Allah is swerving from duty and opposing the truth and taking anything without being prompted by desire is harmony and agreement with truth and discarding it is insincerity and hypocrisy.

THE FORTIETH DISCOURSE

He (may Allah be pleased with him) said
Do not expect to be included in the company of spiritual people unless you have become an enemy of your whole self and have become absolutely separated from all the organs of

your body and all your limbs and have cut off all connections
with your existence, with your movements and restful conditions, with your hearing and seeing, with your speaking and
holding, with your effort and action and your action and your
intelligence and with everything that proceeds from you before
your spiritual existence comes into being in you. And all that
will be found in you after the spiritual existence is breathed
into you because all these things constitute a screen between
you and your Lord. So when you become a soul pure and
simple, secret of secrets and unseen of the unseen, positively
distinct from all things in secret and recognising everything as
an enemy and a screen and darkness, just as Hazrat Ibrahim
(Abraham) alaihissalam Khalilullah (the friend of Allah) may
Allah's peace and blessings be upon him) says :

"So surely they are my enemies excepting the Lord of the
worlds (Who is the only friend." (xxvi-77).

And he said this in respect of the idols. So you should
consider your whole being and your parts, as idols together
with the rest of the creation and should not obey anything out
of them and should not follow it at all. Then you will be confi-
ded with secrets and Divine knowledge and rare things in it and
will be gifted with the power of creation and miracle-working
which is of the type of power to be found in the possession of
believers in heaven.

Then you will be in this condition as if you are resurrected
after death in the hereafter. So you will be wholly a manifestation of the power of Allah ; you will hear through Allah and
see through Allah and speak through Allah and hold through
Allah and walk through Allah and understand through Allah
and will have your comfort and rest through Allah. Thus you
will be blind to everything besides Him, you will be deaf to
everything besides Him : so that you will not find anything
existing besides Him so long as you observe the limits of law
and conform to the injunctions and prohibitions. Then if anything is amiss in you from the requirements of law you should
know that you are being tried and tempted and played with by
the devils. So return to the commandment of Law and stick to
it and keep yourself clear of low desires, because every fact
which is not confirmed by the law is unbelief.

THE FORTY-FIRST DISCOURSE

He (may Allah be pleased with him) said

We shall set forth for you a parable on affluence and we will say, "Do you not see the king taking an ordinary man and making him a governor and putting him the charge of a certain town and giving him the robe of honour and flags and banners and drums and army ; and the man passes some time in this condition till when he feels secure in it and begins to believe in its permanence and to take pride in it and forgets his previous condition and handicaps and humiliation and poverty and obscurity thereof and he is seized with pride and vanity, there comes from the king the order of his dismissal and the king demands an explanation for the crimes he has committed and for his transgressing his injunctions and prohibition. So the king imprisons him in a narrow and dark prison and pro- longs his imprisonment, and the man continues to remain in this suffering and humiliation and poverty in consequence of which his pride and vanity melt and his self is broken and the fire of his desires is extinguished and all this happens before the eyes of the king and within his knowledge, after which he becomes favourably inclined towards the man and looks at him with compassion and mercy and orders his release from the prison together with acts of kindness towards him and robe of honour and the restoration of the governorship and that of another city like this. And he gives all these things to the man as a free gift. So he continues in this state of governorship which remains steady and pure and sufficient and blessed.

So this is the case of a believer when Allah draws him near and chooses him. He opens before his heart's eyes doors of mercy and kindness and reward, so he sees with his heart which no eye has seen and no ear has heard nor which has occurred to any human heart in respect of the study of the unseen things of the kingdom of heavens and earth and of near- ness to Allah and of the sweet and nice word and happy promise and lavish affection and of the acceptance of prayer and truthfulnes and of the fulfilment of promise and the words of great wisdom thrown on his heart which express themselves through his tongue, and along with these He completes on this man His favours externally over his body nd his organs in the shape of food and drink and dress and lawful wife and other permissible things and the paying of regard to the bounds of law and to the formal acts of devotion. So Allah maintains this condition for His believing servant who is drawn towards Him for a considerable time until when the servant feels secure in it and becomes deceived by it and believes in its permanence, Allah opens for him doors of calamity and various kinds of difficulties in respect of life and property and wife and children and removes from him all that He had bestowed upon him before this, so that he is left astonished and helpless and broken down and cut off from his people.

If he looks at his external circumstances he sees things which appear evil to him and if he looks at his own heart and his inner self he sees what grieves him. And if he asks Allah to remove his trouble, his petition does not meet with any accep· tance and if he asks for any good promise he does not get it quickly and if he promises anything he is not informed about its fulfilment and if he sees any dream he does not succeed in interpreting it and getting at its truth and if he intends to get back towards people he does not get any means to it; and if any alternative appears to him and he acts on it he is immediately overtaken by chastisement and the hands of people get hold of his body and their tongues assail his honour, and if he wants to free himself from the obligation or the condition in which he finds himself and to go back to the condition previous to his acceptance, such a prayer is not accepted and if he asks for cheerful submission and delightfulness and happy living in the midst of the calamities with which he is surrounded, even this is not granted.

Then it is that his self begins to melt and the low desires begin to disappear and his intentions and longings begin to pass away and the existence of everything is reduced to naught. So this state of affairs is prolonged for him and even made to increase in intensity and severity and stress, until when the servant passes away altogether from human characteristics and attributes and remains merely a soul, he hears an inner voice calling out to him :

"Urge on with your foot; here is a cool washing place and a drink" (xxxviii-42).

As it was said to Hazrat Ayyub (Job) alaihissalam (peace be upon him). Then Allah makes oceans of His mercy and compassion and tenderness and kind acts to flow into his heart and revives him with His happiness and sweet smell of know-ledge of reality and subtle points of His knowledge and opens for him the doors of His favours and lavish care and extends the hands of people towards him for gift and service in all con-ditions of life and releases the tongues of people for his praise and applause and good renown in every affair and urges the feet of people to come to him and causes the necks of people to bow before him and makes the kings and chiefs subservient to him and completes on him His favours internal and enternal and takes charge of his external upbringing, through His creation and other blessings and perfects his inner upbringing by His kindness and favour, and makes this state continue for him till He meets him. Then He makes him enter in what no eye has seen and no ear has heard nor has it occurred to the heart of any man as Allah says

"No soul knows what is in store for them of that which will refresh the eyes a reward for what they did." (xxxii-17).

THE FORTY-SECOND DISCOURSE

He (may Allah be pleased with him) said

The spirit of man can be in two conditions and there is no third one : the state of happiness and the state of trouble. So when it is in trouble there is anxiety and complaint and displea-sure and criticism and finding fault with Allah, the Mighty, the Exalted, lacking in patience and cheerful submission and recon-cilement; and betraying on the contrary bad manners, sin of associating the creation and worldly means with the Creator, and finally unbelief. Then when it is in comfort it is a victim of greed and insolence and predominance of low desire and enjoyments. Whenever it gratifies on desire it wants another and belittles what it already possesses of blessings; then it finds fault and defect in these blessings and asks for one better than these and brighter as well, out of what is not in its lot and turns away from what is allotted to it and thus involves the man in a long series of troubles and does not feel contented with what is in its hands and what is allotted to it and lands into distress and in places of destruction in the midst of long series of trouble which has no end either in this world or in the hereafter, as it has been said :

"Verily the most distressing of punishments is seeking what is not allotted."

Thus when it is in trouble it does not desire anything except its removal and forgets all pleasures and desires and delightful things and does not ask anything out of these. Then when he is blessed with an easy and comfortable life, he returns to arrogance and greediness and disobedience and recalcitrant turning away from obedience to his Lord and plunges in his sinful occupation. And he forgets the misfortune he had lately been into and the calamity to which he has been a victim.

So he is hurried back to a state worse than what he was in with various kinds of calamities and troubles as a punishment for what it had perpetrated and committed and for major sins, in order to keep him away from these and restrain him from sinful acts in future, after it was found that ease and comfort would not reform him but that his safety lay in calamities and difficulties.

So had he observed good manners when the calamity was removed from him and help fast to obedience and thankfulness and cheerful acceptance of his lot, it would have been better for him in this world and the hereafter. Then you would have obtained an increase in the comforts of life and the pleasure of Allah and happy life and resourcefulness and pleasure.

So whoever desires safey in this world's life and in the hereafter he should cultivate patience and cheerful submission and avoid complaining against people and obtain all his necessities from his Lord, the Mighty, the Glorious, and make it an obligation to obey Him and should wait for ease and be exclusively devoted to Him, the Mighty, the Glorious. He in any case is better than those besides Him in the whole of His creation.

More often than not the deprivation caused by Him is a gift, His punishment a blessing, His calamity a remedy, His promise

a cash. His credit is existing state. His word is a deed. Undoubtedly, His word and His commandment, when He intends to do
anything, is only saying to it "Be," and it comes into being. So
all His actions are good and based on wisdom and expedience,
excepting that He keeps the knowledge of His expedience
hidden from His servants and He is alone in this. So it is better
and proper for the servants to be in a state of cheerful submission and resignation and to be engaged in service to Him by
carrying out His orders and observing His prohibitions and
being resigned to His allotment and by discarding such occupations as pertain to the nourishment of the creation—because
this privilege is the source of all allotments and the point of
their coming into force and their basis; and to be silent on why,
how, and when (of happenings) and to refrain from ascribing
fault to Allah in all His actions and inactions. This statement
derives its validity from a *hadith* narrated by Abdullah Ibn
Abbas may Allah be pleased with him, who is quoted by Ata
Ibn Abbas may Allah be pleased with him. Ibn Abbas is reported to have said:

I was riding behind the Prophet of Allah (peace and blessings
of Allah be upon him) when he said to me, "My boy, guard
the obligations to Allah, Allah will look after you; guard the
obligations to Allah, you will find Him in front of you."

So when you ask from Allah, and when you seek assistance
seek it from Him. The pen is dried after writing down all that
is to happen and if the servants of Allah strive to benefit you
with anything which Allah has not decreed for you they will not
be able to do it and if all the servants of Allah strive to harm
you with anything which Allah has not decreed for you they
will not be able to do so. So if you can act upon the commandments of Allah with sincerity of faith, do it; and if you
are unable to do so then surely it is better to be patient on what
you dislike seeing that there is much good in that. And know
that the help of Allah comes through patience and comfortable
circumstances with distress and that difficulty is accompanied
by ease. So it behoves every believer that he should make this
hadith a mirror for his heart and its internal and external garment and his motto and should act on it in all his actions and

moments of pause so that he may remain safe in this world and
the hereafter and may receive honour in both of them by the
Mercy of Allah, the Exalted.

THE FORTY-THIRD DISCOURSE

He (may Allah be pleased with him) said:
Whoever asks anything from men does so only through his
ignorance of Allah and weakness of faith and knowledge of
reality, and of certainty and lack of patience; and whoever
refrains from asking does so only through abundance of his
knowledge of Allah, the Mighty, the Glorious, and through the
strength of his faith and of certainty and through an incessant
increase in his knowledge of Allah every moment and his
shyness from Him, the Mighty, the Glorious.

THE FORTY-FOURTH DISCOURSE

He (may Allah be pleased with him) said:
Surely every prayer of the man of spiritual knowledge, to
Allah the Mighty, the Glorious, is not granted and every promise
made to him is not redeemed so that he may not meet with
destruction through over-optimism. Because there is no spiritual
state nor any spiritual station but has fear and hope attached to
it. These two are like two wings of a bird, but for which no
flight can be perfect. And this is true of every state and station,
with this much of difference that every state has its corresponding fear and hope. Thus a man of spiritual knowledge enjoys
the nearness of Allah and his state and station is that he does
not wish for anything but Allah and does not incline to and feel
satisfied with anything which is besides Him and is not delighted
with any that is besides Him. Thus the asking (on the part) of
(devotee) for the acceptance of his prayer and the fulfilment of
the promise made to him, is opposed to his path and not in
accordance with his state.

And there are two reasons for this. One is that he may not
be overcome by hope and delusion through the subtle planning
of Allah and become unmindful of the requisite amount of
good behaviour in his approach to Allah and thus meet his

destruction. And the second is that it may amount to associating something with his Lord, the Mighty, the Glorious, which is besided Him. Because there is no one in the world absolutely free from sin, excepting the Prophets. It is for this reason that He does not always grant the prayers and fulfil the promises made to the devotee, lest he should ask anything urged by his own nature without any reference to any obedience to the commandments of Allah wherein lies the chance of polytheism, and there are numerous chances of polytheism (*shirk*) in every state, step and station of a spiritual pilgrim. But when the prayer is in accordance with a commandment, it is a thing which increases a man in his nearness to Allah like prayer and fasting and other things among the obligatory and supererogatory duties of religion, because in this there is obedience to commandment.

THE FORTY-FIFTH DISCOURSE

He (may Allah be pleased with him) said:
Know that people are of two kinds. One kind of people are those that are blessed with the good things of the world, whereas the other kind are tried with what their Lord has decreed for them. As for those who receive the good things, they are not free from the blemishes of sin and darkness in the enjoyment of what they are given. Such a person indulges in luxury on account of these things, when all of a sudden the decree of Allah comes, which darkens his surrounding through various kinds of misfortunes and calamities in the shape of diseases and sufferings and troubles on his own life and property and on the members of his family and on his offspring so that life becomes miserable through them, and it appears as if he had never enjoyed anything. He forgets the comforts and their sweetness. And if the affluence continues together with wealth and position and male slaves and female slaves and security from enemies, he is in a state of blessing as if calamity has no existence for him. And if he is in the midst of calamity it seems as if happiness has no existence. And all this is due to ignorance of his Master.

The if he had known that his Master is absolutely free to do whatever He likes and changes and transforms and sweetens and embitters and enriches and impoverishes and raises and lowers and gives honour and abases and gives life and causes death and gives a man precedence and pushes him to the background—if he had known all this he could not have felt secure in the midst of happy worldly circumstances and could not have felt proud on account of them, nor would he have despaired of happiness while in a state of calamity.

This wrong behaviour of his is due also to his ignorance of this world, which is in reality the place of trials and bitterness and ignorance and pain and darkness, and of which the rule is trial and happiness only an exception. Thus the worldly life is like a tree of aloes of which the first taste is bitter whereas the ultimate consequence is sweet like honey and no man can get at its sweetness unless he first swallowed its bitter taste and no one can reach the honey unless he has first showed patience with its bitterness. So whoever has shown patience on the trials of the world is entitled to taste its blessings.

To be sure, a labourer is given his wages after his forehead has sweated and his body has become tired and his soul has become troubled and his breast has become contracted and his strength has departed and his self has become humiliated and his vanity has become broken through the service of a creature like himself. Thus when one has drunk all this bitterness in full, then follows for him good food and fruits and dress and comforts and joy even if they be small. Thus the world is a thing of which the first part is bitterness like the top part of some honey kept in a vessel mixed with bitterness, so that an eater cannot get to the bottom of the vessel and thus eat the pure honey out of it until after he has tasted the top part of it.

So, when the servant of Allah has persevered in the performance of the commandment of Allah, the Mighty, the Glorious, and in keeping away from His prohibitions and in submitting before Him and in surrendering himself to the decrees of destiny, and when he has drunk the bitterness thereof and has lifted the burden of it and has struggled against his own desires and has discarded his own objectives, Allah gives him, as a result of this, good life and loving attention and comfort and honour, and He becomes his guardian and feeds him just as a suckling baby is fed without any effort on his part

and without his bearing any trouble and strain in this world
and in the hereafter, in the same manner as an eater of the
bitter top part of the aforesaid honey relishes the bottom part
of the contents of the vessel

So it is proper for the servant who has been favoured by
Allah not to feel secure from the trial of Allah by being
enchanted by the favour not to feel sure as to its perpetuity
and thus become forgetful of gratitude for it and relax its
restrictions by discarding thankfulness on account of it. The
Holy Prophet (peace and blessings of Allah be upon him) has
said:

"Happy worldly circumstances is a savage thing: so restrain
it by thankfulness."

Thus thankfulness of the blessing of wealth is to acknowledge
it to the Giver of it Who it bountiful, that is Allah, to mention
it to one's ownself in all conditions of life and to appropriate
His favour and generosity and also that one should not feel
like having any claim on Allah nor should one outstep His
bounds in this matter nor should one discard His commandment in the matter; and after this by fulfilling the obligation
to Him in respect of Zakat and expiation and votive offerings
and alms and by redressing the sufferings of the oppressed ones
and helping the needy who are in difficulty and whose circumstances have changed from good to bad, that is to say. whose
times of happiness and hopefulness have changed into hard
and difficult ones. And thankfulness for the blessing of comfort in the limbs and the organs of the body is to use them in
carrying out the commandments of Allah and in restraining
oneself from things forbidden and from evil and sinful acts

So this is how to protect blessings from passing away and
to irrigate its plant and to accelerate the growth of its branches
and leaves ; and to help the beautification of its fruit and to
sweeten its taste and to assure the safety of its end and to make
its eating tasteful and to make its swallowing easy and to make
it yield comfort and to enable it to maintain its growth in the
body and to make its blessing manifest itself on the organs of
the body through various kinds of acts of obedience to Allah
such as will render one nearer to Allah and keep him in His
remembrance, and will further make the servant enter in the

life hereafter into the mercy of Allah, the Mighty, the Glorious, and will earn for him an abiding life in the gardens of paradise in the holy companionship of Prophets. *Siddiqs* (the truthful ones) and *Shahids* (witnesses) and the *Salihs* (the righteous)—a beautiful company these are.

But if one does not act like this and becomes enamoured of what appears of the outward beauty of such a life and engrossed in the enjoyments of it and becomes contented with the glitter of its mirage and the sparkle of its lightning-like appearance, all of which are like the blowing of cool breeze in the morning of a hot summer day and like the softness of the skin of a serpent and scorpion; and becomes forgetful of the deadly poison which has been reposed in it and of its deep deception and craftiness – all of which have as their aim to catch him and imprison him and to destroy him—such a man should be given the tidings of rejection and of speedy destruction and poverty with abasement and humiliation in this world and of chastisement in the long run in burning hell-fire.

And as for the trial of man—sometimes it comes as a punishment for any violation of law and any sin which has been committed: at others it comes with the object of removing the defects and refining the nature of man, and at still others it comes to raise a man in spiritual rank and to take him to higher stages where he may join the people of spiritual knowledge who have experience of different states and positions, for whom the grace of the Lord of the creation and humanity has been allotted beforehand, who have been made to travel in the fields of calamities riding on the conveyance of tenderness and kindness and whom He has soothed by the breeze of kind observation and loving watch in their movements and repose, because such a trial was not meant for destruction and for hurling them in the depths of hell: on the contrary, by means of these trials Allah has tested them for selection and choice and has brought out from them the reality of faith and has refined it and made it distinct from polytheism and boastings of self and hypocrisy and has made a free gift, as a reward for them, of various kinds of knowledge and secret, and light.

So when these people have become clean outwardly and inwardly and when their hearts have become purified, He has made them among the specially selected and the favourites of His court and companions of His mercy in this world and in the hereafter—in this world through their hearts and in the hereafter through their bodies. Thus the calamities are purifiers of the dirt of polytheism and breakers of connections with people and with the means of the world and with desires and wishes and are instrumental in melting the boastfulness and greediness and the expectation of returns for obedience to commandments in the shape of high positions and stations in paradise and gardens of heaven.

Now, the indication of trial by way of punishment is want of patience on the arrival of these trials and bewailing and complaints before people. And the indication of trial by way of purification and removal of weakness is the presence of graceful patience without any complaint and expression of grief before friends and neighbours and without any disgust with the performance of commandments and acts of obedience. And the indication of trial for the exaltation of rank is the presence of pleasure and amity and composure of mind and peacefulness with regard to the act of Allah, the Lord of the earth and heavens, and to completely lose oneself in this trial till the time of its removal in course of time.

THE FORTY-SIXTH DISCOURSE

He (may Allah be pleased with him) said :

There is a saying of the Holy Prophet (peace and blessings of Allah be upon him) who reports it from his Lord that:

"Whosoever engages himself in My remembrance and has no time to ask anything from Me I give him better than what is given to those who ask for things."

And this is so because when Allah wishes to choose and select a believer for His own purposes, He makes him pass through various spiritual conditions and tries him with various kinds of struggles and calamities. So He makes him poor after affluence and compels him almost to the point of begging from people for his livelihood at times when all the various ways are closed for him ; then saves him from begging for livelihood but compels him almost to the point of borrowing from people. Then He saves him from borrowing as well but compels him to work for his livelihood and makes it easy for him. Then he lives by his earning which is after the example of the Holy Prophet (may Allah's peace and blessings be upon him).

But then He makes earning hard for him and commands him by revelation to beg from people and this is a secret commandment which is known and recognised by the person concerned. And He makes this begging an act of devotion for him and makes it sinful to discard it and this in order that his vanity may disappear thereby and his ego be smashed and this is a state of spiritual exercise. And his begging is under Divine compulsion and not by way of polytheism. Then He saves him from this and commands him to take to borrowing from people by an absolute commandment which it is not possible to escape from, as was the case with the previous kind of begging.

Then He changes him from this condition and severs him from people and makes his livelihood dependent on his asking it from Him. So he asks each and everything that he needs from Allah and He gives it to him and does not give anything if he keeps silent and refrains from praying for it.

Then He changes him from the state of asking by tongue to that of asking by heart. So he asks from Him everything that he needs by heart. And He gives him everything that he needs, so much so that if he asks by his tongue He does not give it to him or if he begs from people they either do not give anything to him.

Then He makes him disappear completely both from himself as well as from begging either in open or in secret. Then He rewards him with everything that puts right and reforms man,—from among things that are eaten and drunk and worn and constitute other requirements of human life without his making an effort for it or without even the thought of it crossing his mind. Then He befriends him and this is in accordance with the saying:

"Surely my friend and guardian is Allah who has revealed the Book and He befriends the righteous people." (xii-196).

And now the word received from Allah by the Holy Prophet (peace of Allah be on him) becomes demonstrated in fact, namely, "who has no time for asking anything I give him more than what I have given to those who have asked," and this is the state of merging in Allah and a state which belongs to the ordinary saints as well as *Abdal*. At this stage he is given the power of creation and all that he needs comes to exist by the permission of Allah and to this effect there is a word of His in a Book of His :

O son of Adam ! I am Allah, there is no God excepting Me; I say to a thing "Be" and it comes to exist. Obey Me, so that if you say to a thing "Be" it likewise will come to exist.

THE FORTY-SEVENTH DISCOURSE

He (may Allah be pleased with him) said :

An old man asked me in my dream saying : "What makes a servant of Allah near to Allah ?" I said : "This process has a beginning and an end, so the beginning of it is piety and chastity and its end is to be pleased with Allah and to surrender oneself to His way and to rely on Him entirely."

THE FORTY-EIGHTH DISCOURSE

He (may Allah be pleased with him) said :

It beseems a believer that he should first attend to the obligatory duties. And when he has accomplished them he should attend to the *Sunnah* or the practice of the Holy Prophet (may Allah's peace and blessings be upon him) And it is only when he has finished with these that he should take to the optional and extra duties. So when a man has not performed his obligatory duties, if he attends to the *Sunnah* it will be foolishness and stupidity and if he attends to the *Sunnah* and *Nafal* or supererogatory duties before he has performed his obligatory duties it will not be accepted of him and he will be based. So, his example is like the example of a man who is asked by the king to serve him but he does not come to him (king) and stays to serve the chief who is the slave of the king and his servant and is under his power and sovereignty. It is reported by Hazrat Ali son of Abu Talib (Allah be pleased with

him), that the Holy Prophet (peace and blessings of Allah be
upon him) said

"The instance of a man who says supererogatory prayers
while he is in arrears with reward to his obligatory prayers is
like the instance of a pregnant woman who carries but when
she approaches the time of delivery she aborts. Thus she no
longer remains pregnant nor does she become a mother."

Similar is the case of the praying man from whom Allah
does not accept supererogatory prayers so long as he has not
performed his obligatory prayers. Also the instance of a man
who prays is like that of a business man who cannot have any
profit unless he has first laid his hand on the capital. Similarly,
if a man says supererogatory prayers, these will not be accepted
of him unless he has first attended to his obligatory prayers.
And same is the case of one who discards the *Sunnah* and takes
to supererogatory prayers such as have not been included in
the obligatory duties nor have they been clearly stated and
emphasised by any order. So among the obligatory duties is
the discarding of unlawful things, of associating anything with
Allah, of taking exception to His dispensation and decrees, of
responding to people's voice and following their wishes and of
turning away from the commandment of Allah and from obedience to Him. The Holy Prophet (peace and blessings of Allah
be upon him) has said : "No obedience is due to any man
where sinning against Allah is involved."

THE FORTY-NINTH DISCOURSE

He (may Allah be pleased with him) said :
Whoever prefers sleep to the spending of night in wakeful
prayer which is the cause of alertness chooses an inferior thing
and the one which attaches him to the dead and makes him
indifferent towards all occupations because sleep is the brother
of death. It is therefore that sleep is unbecoming of Allah
because He is free from all defects. And in the same way sleep
cannot be predicated of the angels because they remain very
near to Allah, the Mighty, the Glorious. And similarly sleep
cannot be associated with the people of heaven because they are

in very exalted and holy, decent and honourable positions, and because that will cause defect in their condition of life. Thus all good lies in keeping awake and all evil lies in sleep and indifference towards work.

So whoever eats out of greed, eats too much, and drinks too much and also sleeps too much, much that is good disappears from him. And whoever eats even a little from unlawful things is like one who has eaten a lot from permissible things out of greed because an unlawful thing beclouds the faith and darkens it. So when faith is darkened there is no prayer and no worship and no sincerity. And whoever eats a lot from lawful things under the commandment of Allah becomes like one who has eaten a little in the joy of worship and strength. So a lawful thing is a light added unto light whereas an unlawful thing is darkness added unto darkness in which there is nothing good ; so the eating of a lawful thing out of greed and without any reference to commandment is like the eating of an unlawful thing in a way and it brings sleep in which there is no good.

THE FIFTIETH DISCOURSE

He (may Allah be pleased with him) said

The state of your affairs can be either the one or the other of the following two :

(1) Either you are not in the nearness of Allah, the Mighty, the Glorious, or

(2) You are close to Him.

Now if you are away from Him, how is it that you are sitting idle and are remiss in obtaining your large share and blessing and abiding honour and plentifulness and security and self-sufficiency and lavish care in this world and in the hereafter. So get up and hasten in your flight towards Him with your two wings. One of these wings is renunciation of enjoyments and of unlawful desires for them and of permissible things and all comforts ; the other is bearing of pain and unpleasant things and to embark on difficult adventures and to get away from people and desires and wishes in this world and in the hereafter

so as to be successful in union with Allah and nearness to Him,
then you will get all that a man may desire and obtain. You
will then have great exaltation and honour. And if you are
among those who have been honoured with His kindness and
whom His love has absorbed and who have received His mercy
and compassion, then show the best of manners and do not
be puffed up with the thought of the state you are in, lest you
should become negligent of your service and should lean
towards the original arrogance, ignorance and oppression and
hastiness. There is a word of Allah in this connection :
      "And man bore it, surely he is unjust and ignorant".
(xxxiii-72).
      Again : "And man is ever hasty" (xvii-11).
      And protect your heart from being inclined towards what
you have renounced of people and desires and wishes and
option and effort and from losing patience and harmony and
pleasure with Allah at the time of the befalling of calamity but
throw yourself before Him in the manner of a ball before a
polo-player who makes it revolve by his stick or like a dead
body in front of a man who gives it the funeral bath or like a
suckling baby in the lap of mother or nurse. Be blind to what
is besides Him so that you do not see anything but Him—
nothing that exists, neither any harm, nor any benefit, nor any
gift, nor any withholding of a gift. Consider the people and
the worldly means at the time of suffering and calamity as
lashes from Him, the Mighty, the Glorious, with which He
strikes you and consider them at the time of comfort and ease
and gift as His hand that is feeding you.

THE FIFTY-FIRST DISCOURSE

      He (may Allah be pleased with him) said :
      The man of piety receives his reward twice by way of his
portion. First on account of his renouncing the world so that
he does not take to it on account of his desire nor in com-
pliance with the urges of his own self but it is just to fulfil the
commandment of Allah that he has anything to do with it.
So when his enmity with his own self and opposition to his

desires are established and he is counted among the verifiers of truth and friends of Allah and he is admitted in the company of *Abdal* and *Arifin* (knowers of truth), it is then that he is commanded to take to the world and establish contact with it, because now there is a portion for him in it which cannot be discarded and which has not been created for any other person, and after the recording of which the pen of destiny has become dried and about which the knowledge of Allah has gone beforehand. Then when the commandment has been fulfilled he takes his share of the world or, receiving information about the knowledge of Allah, he establishes contact with the world to act as the vehicle of the destiny appointed by him and of His action in the matter, without his being involved in it and without any desire or purpose and effort on his part—he is rewarded on account of these for the second time, because he does all these things in obedience to the commandment or to be in accord with the act of Allah in the matter.

Then if it be said—how did you make the statement about reward in connection with one who has been in a very high spiritual position and who, according to your own description, has been admitted in the category of the *Abdal* and *Arifin* and who has been among those accepted by Allah, having vanished from people and their own selves and from desires and purposes and enjoyments and wishes and expectations of rewards on account of their deeds—people who see in all their acts of obedience and worship nothing but acts of Allah and His mercy and His blessing and His backing and provisions of ease from Him and who believes that they are nothing but the humble servants of Allah and that a servant has no right as against his master, seeing that his person and his movements and his reposes and his efforts are all possessions of his master : how then can it be said in relation to such a person that he is rewarded, seeing that he does not ask for any reward or anything else in exchange for his action and does not see any action as proceeding from him but considers himself among the worthless people and among the poorest of the poor in respect of deeds ? If it be so said, the reply would be : "You have spoken the truth, excepting that Allah bestows His grace on him and nourishes him with fond care with His blessing and brings him up with His kindness and tender care and mercy and favour, when he has restrained his hand from the affairs, of his own self and from asking for its enjoyments which are reserved for the after-life and from deriving and benefit out of it and from warding off any harm arising out of it. So much so that he becomes like a suckling baby which has no movement in the affairs of his self and who is nurtured with fond care with the grace of Allah and sustenance provided by Him at the hands of his parents, who are his guardians and sureties.

When He has taken away from him all interest in his own affairs He makes the hearts of people incline towards him and infuses His mercy and compassion in the hearts so much so that everyone becomes kind to him and becomes inclined to him and does him a good turn. And in this way everything besides Allah becomes such as does not move but with His commandment and, in response to His act and the grace of Allah, attends him in this world and in the hereafter nurturing him in both and keeping away from him all suffering. So it is that the Holy Prophet (peace and blessings of Allah be upon him) says :

"Surely my friends is Allah who has revealed the Book and He befriends the good". (vii-196).

THE FIFTY-SECOND DISCOURSE

He (may Allah be pleased with him) said:
Certainly Allah tries a party from the believers who are His friends and who hold friendly relations with Him and spiritual knowledge in their possession, in order that they may be turned through the trial towards prayer to Him and He loves to receive prayers from them. Then when they pray He loves to accept their prayer so that He may give generosity and munificence their rightful shares because these two ask Allah, the Mighty and Glorious, at the time of the prayer of the believer, for acceptance and sometimes the acceptance is granted but not the immediate fulfilment of prayer, on account of the deferment of decree and not on account of non-acceptance or deprivation. So

the servant of Allah should show good manner at the time of
the befalling of a calamity and investigate into his own sins of
neglecting commandments or being guilty of doing forbidden
things, both open and secret, or of finding fault with the decree
of Providence, for more often than not he becomes involved in
such a trial as a punishment for such sins. So if the calamity is
removed well and good or else he should continue to pray and
show humility and make apology and also persist in his petition
to Allah, for it is possible that the trial is meant to make him
persist in his prayer and petition; and he should not blame
Allah for thus delaying the fulfilment of prayer in the manner
we have already discussed.

THE FIFTY-THIRD DISCOURSE

He (may Allah be pleased with him) said:

Ask from Allan pleasure with His decree or the ability to be
merged in the action of the Lord because in this lies great comfort and unique high heaven in this world and it is also a big
gate of Allah and a means to the love of Allah for the believing
slave. So whomsoever Allah loves He does not chastise him in
this world nor in the hereafter. In these two virtues lie the contact with Allah, union with Him and an intimate connection
with Him. And do not be engrossed in your efforts for the
pleasures of this life and for such shares as are either not allotted
to you or are so allotted. So if they are not allotted it is foolishness and stupidity and ignorance to make efforts in obtaining
them and it is also the greatest of all punishments as it has been
said:

"Among the greatest of punishments is to strive for what is
not allotted by Providence."

And if it is allotted it is nothing but agreed and divided
loyalty in the matter of servitude and love and truth, to be
engrossed in its pursuit because engrossment in anything which
is not Allah, the Mighty, the Glorious, is polytheism. And one
who strives for worldly pleasure is not sincere in his love for
and friendship to Allah, so whoever adopts with Allah anything
other than 'Him is a liar.

Similarly, one who looks forward to any return for his action
is insincere. Sincere is he who serves Allah just to give *Rabubiyya*,
i.e. the attribute of Allah that controls and nourishes the
universe, its due. Such a person serves Him on account of His
mastership and deservingness in as much as Allah, the Mighty,
the Glorious, is his owner and it is incumbent on him to perform virtuous deeds and be obedient to Him, seeing that he
wholly belongs to Him together with his movements and restful
states and all his various efforts and struggles. And the servant
and all that he possesses belongs to his Master. And how can it
be otherwise? For, as we have already stated elsewhere all acts
of servitude are a blessing of Allah and His favour on His
servant because it is He who gives him the power for their performance and has given him power over them.

So to be busy with the expression of gratitude to Him is
better and preferable to asking for returns and rewards from
Him on account of such actions.

Then how.can you get engrossed in striving for the pleasure
of the world when you have seen how a large number of people,
whenever pleasures of worldly life multiply in their possession
and the enjoyments and the worldly comforts that are allotted
to them come in incessantly and without any break, their resentment towards their Lord and their disgust and ingratitude in
respect of the blessings increase and their grief and anxiety and
neediness for things not allotted to them and consequently not
in their possession, multiply? And their own share of worldly
things which is with them appears paltry and small and
loath-some and the worldly things which belong to others
appear great and beautiful to their hearts and eyes and they
begin to make efforts to obtain them in spite of the fact that
they are not allotted to their share. In this way passes away
their life and their powers become exhausted and they become
old and their wealth disappears and their bodies become tired
and their foreheads sweat and the records of their life become
darkened by excess of their sins and by their commission of big
offences in pursuing things which are allotted to others and
by their negligence to the commandments of their Lord. So they
do not succeed in getting these things and make an exit from this
worldly

life as poor men, neither being one way nor the other, losers
in this life and in the hereafter, not thinking their Lord for
what He has allotted to them of their share and therefore
seeking His assistance on account of them in acts of obedience
to Him. And they do not obtain what they strive for from
the share of others but only waste their worldly life as well
as the one hereafter; so they are the worst of people and most
ignorant and vilest in intelligence and insight.

So had they become pleased with the decree of Providence
and remained contented with His gift and been obedient to Him
in the best manners, their own share of this worldly life must
have come to them without any effort and anxiety; then they
would have been taken in the neighbourhood of Allah, the
Exalted, and would have received from Him all that they
desired and wished for. May Allah make us and you among
those who have become pleased with His decree and who have
made this their prayer that they may merge in His will and
acquire safety of their spiritual health and strength to do what
He likes and is pleased with.

THE FIFTY-FOURTH DISCOURSE

He (may Allah be pleased with him) said:
Whosoever desires the life hereafter it is incumbent one him
to be indifferent towards the world, and whosoever desires Allah
it is incumbent on him that he should be indifferent towards
the life hereafter. Thus he should discard his worldly life for the
sake of his Lord. So as long as any desire from among the
desires of this world continues to exist in his heart and any
relish from among the relishes of it and any effort for comfort
from among the comforts of it in regard to various things of
food and drink and dress and marriage and residence and
conveyance and rulership and chieftainship and advancement in
his knowledge of various branches of learning and of jurisprudence in preference to five institutions of worship and to the
narration of Hadith (i.e. reported sayings and acts of the Holy
Prophet (may Allah's peace and blessings be upon him) and the
recitation of the Quran with its varied readings and syntax and

lexicography and rhetoric, as also the desire for the disappearance of poverty and appearance of affluence and the
departure of calamity and the coming of comfort and in everything the removal of difficulty and coming of benefit—if such a
desire lingers in the mind of a person he is certainly not a pious
man, because in every one of these things there is relish and
pleasure for the self of man and harmony with the desire of
flesh and comfort of the mind and love for it and these things
constitute worldly life in which one loves to remain for good
and with which one tries to get composure of mind and satisfaction.

It beseems on to strive for the expulsion of all these things
from the heart and prepare oneself to remove all these and to
root them out from the mind and to cultivate pleasure in
annihilation and abiding poverty and neediness so that there
does not remain in his heart so much as the pleasure of the
sucking of the stone of a date, and so that his abstemiousness in
worldly life may become pure.

So when he has perfected it, all grief and sorrow from his
heart and all anxiety from his mind will disappear and their will
come to him comforts and goodly life and intimacy with Allah,
as has been said by the Holy Prophet (peace and blessings of
Allah be upon him):

"Indifference towards the world brings happiness to the
heart and body."

But so long as there remains in his heart any attraction for
this world, sorrows and griefs and fear and apprehension will
have a standing abode in his heart and abasement will be a
necessary concomitant for him as also the state of being veiled
from Allah, the Mighty, the Glorious, and from His nearness,
by a veil thick in several folds. So all these will not be removed
except through the complete disappearance of the love of this
world and by the cutting asunder of all connections with it.

Next he should be indifferent towards the life hereafter so
as not to wish for ranks and high grades and beautiful maidens
and handsome boys and houses and mansions and conveyance
and suits of clothes and ornaments and articles of food and
drink and other things of this kind from among what Allah, the
Great, has kept prepared for His believing servants.

So he should not try to get any recompense and reward for his action from Allah, the Mighty, the Glorious, at all this world or in the hereafter. It is only then that he will find Allah giving the full measure of his account as an act of grace from Himself and as a kindness. So He will draw him near Himself and will lavish His kindness on him and He will make Himself known to him with various kindness and acts of goodness, as it is His practice to do with His Prophets and Messengers and with His *Awliya* and His favourites and friends, possessed of knowledge of Him. So the servant becomes every day more and more improved in regard to his affairs throughout his life and then he is transferred to the abode of the hereafter to experience "what no eye has seen, no ear has heard and which has not occurred to any human mind," which in fact surpasses all understanding and which no explanation suffices to cover.

THE FIFTY-FIFTH DISCOURSE

He (may Allah be pleased with him) said:

The enjoyments of life are discarded thrice. In the beginning the servant of Allah goes on in the darkness of his ignorance and in a distracted condition, acting freely by the urges of his nature in all the various circumstances, without any attitude of service towards his Lord and without any rein of religious law to control him and without any limits where to stop by His order. While he is in this state Allah looks to him with the eye of mercy, so He sends him an admonisher from among the people, one who is a righteous servant of His and a counterpart of this admonisher is also found in his own self So both these admonishers become victorious over his self and nature and admonition produces effect on his mind. Then the defect of what is in him such as his riding the conveyance of his own nature and his opposition to truth—becomes manifest. So he inclines towards the law of Allah in all his activities.

Thus the servant of Allah becomes a Muslim standing by the law of Allah, vanishing from his own nature and giving up the unlawful things of the world as also those that are of doubtful nature and the help of people. So he takes to true permissible things and things made lawful by law in all questions of food and drink and dress and marriage and residence and all other affairs; and all this is unavoidable in protecting the foundations of physical health and in deriving strength for obedience to Allah, so that one may receive in full the share allotted to him and beyond which one cannot go—and there is no getting away from this worldly life before having access to it and obtaining it and completing it.

So he travels on the conveyance of permissible and lawful things in conditions of his life so much so that this conveyance takes him to the highest of *Wilayat* and gives him an entry into the company of the verifiers of truth and chosen people possessed of firm resolution who are desirous of the reality which is Allah. So he eats with His order, then· he (the pilgrim) hears a voice from Allah within himself, saying, "Discard your ownself and come: discard enjoyments and the creation if you want the Creator and put off both your shoes of this world and of the hereafter and be empty of all existences and of things which will be created in future and of all desires. And be devoid of all and vanish from everything. And be happy with the unity of Allah and the discarding of polytheism and with the sincerity of purpose. Then enter the vast expanse of Divine nearness with your head bent low out of reverence and do not look right towards the life hereafter nor left towards the worldly life nor yet towards the people nor yet still towards enjoyments."

Then when he attains this stage and his arrival there becomes an established fact he receives the robe of honour from Allah and is covered with lights of honour and various kinds of favour. Then it is said to him, "Dress yourself with blessings and favours and do not be ill-mannered so as to reject and discard desires because the rejection of the gifts of the king amounts to putting pressure on him and slighting his august power. "Then he becomes wrapped up in His favour and allotment without his playing any part in the matter. And before this he used to be coverd in his desires and urges of the self. So it will be said to him. "Cover yourself with the blessings and favours of Allah."

So for him there are four states in attaining the enjoyments. and allotments. The first state is that of the urges of nature:

and this is unlawful. The second state is of the law and this is permissible and lawful. And the third state is that of inner commandment and this is the state of *Wilayat* and discarding of desires. And the fourth state is that of Divine favour, and this is the state of disappearance of purpose and attainment of *Badaliyya* and of being the (Divine) objective, standing by the decree of Destiny, which is the act of Allah, and this is the state of knowledge and of being possessed of the quality of righteousness and no one can be called really righteous unless he has attained this position.

And this accords with the word of Allah :

"Surely my friend is Allah who has revealed the Book and He befriends the righteous people." (xii. 196).

So he is a servant who is restrained from utilising anything of use and benefit to himself and from rejecting anything that harms and causes mischief to him. He becomes like a sucking baby in the hands of its nurse or like a dead body that is being washed by one who is giving it a funeral bath. So the hand of Providence under takes his upbringing without his having any choice in the matter and without any effort on his part, he disappearing from all these things, and not having any state nor any position nor yet any purpose but standing by the decree of Destiny, who sometimes puts him in restraint and at others makes him feel at ease and sometimes makes him rich and at others makes him poor. And he makes no choice nor does he entertain any desire for the passing of any state and change in it. On the contrary, he shows abiding pleasure and eternal concord. And this is the last point of spiritual state which is obtained by *Abdal* and *Awliya*.

THE FIFTY-SIXTH DISCOURSE

He (may Allah be pleased with him) said :

When the servant of Allah has vanished from creation and desire and from his own self and purpose and wishes of this world and of the hereafter, he does not want anything excepting Allah, the Mighty, the Glorious, and everything goes out from his heart. It is then that he attains Allah who selects him and chooses him and loves him and makes him loved by the creation and also makes him such that he loves Him as well as His nearness and receives His favour through His grace and rolls in His blessings. And He throws open on him the doors of His mercy and promises to him that He will never shut them against him. So the servant then adopts Allah, the Mighty, the Glorious, and intends by His intention and devises means by His devising and wills a thing by His will and feels pleased by His pleasure and carries out His commandment and not anyone else's and does not see any existence excepting His, the Mighty, the Glorious, nor any act. Then it beseems that Allah makes him a promise and does not manifest its fulfilment to his servant and the thing which the servant expects in this connection may not come to him and this is because the separateness disappears with the disappearance of desire and purpose and of the seeking of enjoyments. Then his whole self becomes the very act of Allah, the Mighty, the Glorious, and His object. So neither promise nor breach of promise can be spoken of in this connection because this kind of thing can be attributed to one who has desire and purpose. At this stage the promise of Allah, the Mighty, the Glorious, in respect of such a person, can be illustrated by the example of a man who intends within his own self to do a certain thing, then turns the same intent towards something else in the same way as Allah the Mighty, the Glorious, has revealed to our Prophet Muhammad (peace and blessings of Allah be upon him) with regard to revelations abrogating and abrogated as in the words :

"Whatever communications We abrogate or cause to be forgotten We bring one better than it or like it. Do you not know that Allah has power over all things?" (ii. 106).

When the Holy Prophet (peace and blessings of Allah be upon him) cleaned of desire and purpose excepting on certain occasions which Allah has mentioned in the Holy Quran such as in the case of the prisoners on the day of Battle of Badr as in the following words :

"You desire the frail goods of this world, while Allah desires for you the hereafter ; and He is Mighty, Wise. Were it not for an ordinance from Allah that had already gone forth, surely there would have befallen you a great chastisement for what you had taken to". (viii. 67-68).

And he the (Holy Prophet) was the object of Allah, whom he would not leave in one condition and in one thing and in one promise but He would shift him towards the decree of Destiny and leave the rein of Destiny to be handled by him ; so He would move him and make him roll in the midst of Destiny and keep him alert by His words :

"Do you not know that Allah has power over everything?." (ii. 106).

In other words, certainly you are in the ocean of His decreed Providence, the waves of which toss you sometimes this way and sometimes that. So the terminus of the affairs of the *Wali* is the starting point of the affairs of the Holy Prophet (may Allah's peace and blessings be upon him). There is no stage after *Wilayat* and *Badaliyyat* excepting the stage of *Nabuwwat*.

THE FIFTY-SEVENTH DISCOURSE

He (may Allah be pleased with him) said :

All the different states of spiritual experiences are states of restraint because the *Wali* is commanded to look after them. And whatever is ordered to be looked after brings restraint. And standing by the decree of Providence is invariably a state of ease, because there is nothing there which one is commanded to look after excepting his own being in existence in the decree of Destiny. So it is necessary that the *Wali* should not dispute in the matter of the decree of Destiny. He should rather be in accord and not make any contention in regard to all that may happen to him, whether it be sweet or bitter. The states of experience are limited, so it is commanded that the limits should be. guarded. On the other hand, the act of Allah, which is destiny, has no limits that are to be guarded.

And the indication that the servant of Allah has attained the station of Destiny and act of Allah and that of ease is that he is commanded to ask for enjoyments after it is being com-manded to discard them and keep away from them, because when his inside is emptied of enjoyments and nothing remains in him excepting the Lord, he is made at ease and is command- ed to ask and long for and want things that are his portion and which he is sure to receive and attain by his asking for them, so that his dignity in the sight of Allah and his position and the favour of Allah, the Mighty, the Glorious, in the acceptance of his prayer, may become established facts. And to use one's tongue for asking in the matter of gifts of enjoy- ments are mostly indications of case after restraint and exit from all states of experience and stations and from the strains of keeping within the bounds.

And if it be objected that this disappearance of the difficulty of keeping the law leads to atheism and exit from Islam and to dismissal of His word : "And serve your Lord till death comes to you" (xv. 9‘·), my reply would be that this does not mean that and does not lead to that but that Allah is very generous and His friend is very dear to Him so much so that He cannot allow him to occupy a position of defect and one that is ugly in the eye of His law and religion. On the contrary, He saves him from all that has been discussed and turns him away from them and protects him and keeps him alert and directs him to the keeping of the bounds of law. So he acquires protection against sin and keeps within the bounds of the law without any effort and struggle from himself, while he is not conscious of this performance on account of his being in the nearness of his Lord, the Mighty, the Glorious. Allah says :

"Thus (it was) that We might turn away from him civil and indecency; surely he was one of Our sincere servants." (xii. 24).

And he also says :

"Surely as regards My servants you have no authority over them." (xv. 42).

And He also says :

"Save the servants of Allah; the purfied ones." (xxxvii-40).

O poor man ! such a person is held aloft by Allah and is His object, and He nourishes him in the lap of His nearness and His kindness. How can the devil approach him and how can evil and disagreeable things get near him ? How is it that

you keep away from nourishment and pay your homage to
position ? You have said a bad thing. May such a vile and
mean courage and faulty intelligence and wrong distracted
opinion be destroyed by his all comprehensive power and
perfect kindness and wide mercy! And may He cover us by
coverings that are perfect and able to keep off sins and to
protect us and may He nourish us by His perfect blessings and
abiding favours through His spontaneous act of kindness!

THE FIFTY-EIGHTH DISCOURSE

He (may Allah be pleased with him) said :
Be blind to all sides and do not open your eyes to anything
of them. And so long as you look at any one of them, the side
of the favour of Allah, the Mighty, the Glorious, and of His
nearness, will not be opened to you. So close all the sides
with your realisation of the unity of Allah and with the effacement of your self, then with your fading away and your own
effacement and that of your knowledge. Then will be opened
to the eye of your heart the side of Allah, the Mighty, the
Great, and you will see it with the two eyes of your heart when
it comes with the rays of the light of your heart and your faith
and your settled conviction. At that time there will appear a
light from your inside and manifest itself on your outside in
the manner of the light of a lamp which is in a dark night
appearing through its orifices and loopholes and the outside of
the house becomes illuminated by the light of the inside. So
the self and the organs of the body will feel at ease with the
promise of Allah and His gift, to the exclusion of the gifts of
others besides Him and of promise of others besides Him.
So have mercy on our own self and do not be unjust to it
and do not throw it in the darkness of your ignorance and
your foolishness, so as to look at the sides of creation and of
might, of power and of acquisition and of means, and so as to
rely on them. For if you do that all the sides will be closed
against you and the side of the favour of Allah will not be
opened to you by way of chastisement and retribution, on
account of your polytheism in looking up to something besides
Him. So when you have realised His unity and looked at His

favour and placed your hopes on Him to the exclusion of all others and have made yourself blind to all excepting Him, He will make you close and near to Himself and will show His mercy to you and will nourish you and feed you and give you drink and give you medical treatment and make you comfortable and bestow gifts on you and make you opulent and help you and will make you a ruler and make you vanish from the creation and from your own self and make you disappear, so that after this you will see neither your poverty nor your affluence.

THE FIFTY-NINTH DISCOURSE

He (may Allah be pleased with him) said :

Your condition must be either of the following two. It will either be a state of calamity or of blessing. So if it be a state of calamity you should ask therein for patience even with effort —and this is an inferior state—and patience proper and it is a higher state than the other. Then you should ask for pleasure with the decree of Allah and concord with it and finally to be merged in it ; and this is a state befitting the *Abdal* and men of spiritual knowledge, people of knowledge of Allah, the Mighty, the Glorious. And if it be a state of blessing you should ask in it thankfulness on account of it. And thankfulness can be through the tongue and through the heart and through the organs of the body.

The thankfulness of the tongue consists of acknowledging that the blessing is from Allah and of avoiding ascribing it to the people or to your own self or to your might or to your power or to your movement or to your effort or to anything or anybody else besides you, through whose hands it had to pass, because you yourself and they are only the means and instruments for it. The real allotter and executor and creator of it and the actor in the affair and one who is the prime mover of it is Allah, the Mighty. the Glorious. The allotter is Allah and the executor is Allah and the creator is Allah. So He is more deserving of thanks than others. For example one does not look towards the slave who carries a present but towards

the master, the sender of the gift. Allāh says in respect of one
who lacks in this correct attitude :

"They know the outward of his world's life and of the hereafter they are absolutely heedless." (xxx-7).

So whoever looks to the outside and the cause and his
knowledge does not go beyond these, is ignorant and defective
in his intelligence. The term "intelligent" applies to a person
on account of his insight into the ultimate end of things. Thankfulness of the heart consists in believing with the firmest standing conviction that all that is with you of the blessings, benefits
and enjoyments, poses, are from Allah the Mighty, the Glorious,
and not from anyone else. And your thankfulness by tongue
will express what is in your heart as He has :

"And whatever favour is bestowed on you is by Allah".
(xvi-53).

He further says :

"And (He) made complete to you His favours outwardly and
inwardly" (xxxi-20).

Again He says :

''And if you count Allah's favours, you will not be able to
number them". (xiv-34).

So with all these statements there can be no bestower of
favours for a Muslim but Allah. Then the thankfulness
of the organs of the body consists in exercising and using them
in obeying His commandments to the exclusion of all others in
the creation. So you should not respond to anyone among
the creation for anything in which there is any opposition to
Allah, and creation in this connection includes your own self
and your desires and purposes and your wishes and everything
else. Make obedience to Allah the primary thing under which
every other thing should come and make it the guiding factor
and make whatever is besides this as of secondary and subordinate consideration. And if you act differently you will be
deviating from the right course and will prove an unjust person
and will be commanding without the command of Allah issued
for His believing servants and will be following the way which
is not the way of righteous people. Allah, the Mighty, the
Glorious, says :

"And whoever did not judge by what Allah revealed those
are they that are the unjust". (v-45).

And elsewhere it is written : "They are the transgressors"
(v-47).

In that case your destination will be the fire of which the
fuel are the people and the stones.   And when you cannot bear
fever for one hour in this world and cannot bear very small
splinters of fire in it, how will you bear for eternity the hell in
the company of its inmates ? So run away, run away ; make
haste, seek refuge of Allah, seek refuge of Allah.

Guard both the aforesaid states together with their conditions because you cannot be free from either of them for the
whole of your life—either the state of calamity or the state of
happiness.   And give each state its right to your patience and
thankfulness according as I have described to you. So do not
complain in the state of calamity to anyone from among the
people and by no means express your annoyance to anyone
and do not blame your Lord in your mind and do not doubt
His wisdom and His choice of the best thing for you in your
worldly life and in your life hereafter.   And neither should you
go in your zeal to anyone among the people for the purpose of
finding an escape because that will be your associating something with him.

No one shares anything in His possession and no one is able
to harm or to give benefit or to remove difficulties or to
procure anything or to cause illness and bring about calamity
and restore to health and confer anything good excepting Him.
So do not be taken up by the creation either outwardly or
inwardly for they will never avail you anything against Allah.
But stick to patience and pleasure with Allah and harmony
with Him, and absorption in His action.

So if you are deprived of all these blessings it becomes
incumbent on you to call to Him for help and show humiliation and to acknowledge your sins and to complain to Him of
the evil of your self and against your keeping away from truth
and to profess to Him His unity together with His blessings
and proclaim your dissociation from polytheism and harmony
till the writing of Destiny attains its fulness of time and the

calamity disappears and grief is removed and there comes the favour of Allah and ease and relief and happiness, as it came in the case of Hazrat Ayyub (Job) alaihissalam the Prophet of God ; in the same way as the darkness of night goes away and whiteness of the day comes and the coldness of the winter disappears and the breeze of spring comes with its sweet small. Because for everything there is an opposite and contrary and an end and a goal. So patience is its key and its beginning and its end and its guarantee of welfare. And this is as it has been related in the traditions of the Holy Prophet, viz. "Patience is to the faith as the head is to the body." And in another narration : "Patience is the whole of faith."

And sometimes thankfulness comes through the enjoyment of Allah's favours and this is a portion of it that is allotted to you. So your thankfulness is to enjoy it in the state of your self-effacement and of vanishing away of your desires and of your zeal for the preservation and guarding of the bounds of law ; and this is the farthest point of advancement. Take lesson from what I have mentioned to you. You will be guided if Allah the Exalted so wills.

THE SIXTIETH DISCOURSE

He (may Allah be pleased with him) said

The beginning of spiritual life (spiritual journey) is to get out of the natural urges into the path of law and then into the destiny and still onward to be back to the natural urges but on condition of the preservation of the law. So you should get out of your urges of nature in the matter of food and drink and dress and marital relations and place of residence and tendencies and habits, into the injunctions and prohibitions of law. You are to follow the Book of Allah and the practice of His Prophet (blessings and peace of Allah be upon him), as Allah says :

"And accept what the Prophet has brought to you and refrain from what he forbids you to do." (lix-7).

He also says :

"Say : If you love Allah follow me and Allah will love you." (iii-31).

So you will be made to vanish from your desires and your
self and your disobedience both outwardly and inwardly ; then
there will remain nothing in your inside excepting the unity
of Allah and nothing in your outside excepting obedience and
servitude to Allah in what He has enjoined and forbidden. So
this will remain in your manner and way and a kind of garment
for you in your movements and restful conditions, during your
nights and your days and in your journey, and when you are at
home and in your difficulties and in your ease and when you
are in good health and when you are suffering from bad health
and in all your conditions.

Then you will be carried to the valley of Destiny and you
will be controlled by Destiny. Then you will vanish from your
efforts and your struggle and from your power and your
strength and portions will be brought to you the writing of
which has rendered the pen dry and the knowledge of which
has gone before hand. Then you will be partakers in these
portions and will be given protection and safety in their midst
and the boundaries of law will be preserved in them and harmony with the act of Allah will be obtained therein and the
regulation of law will not be broken so as to make the unlawful thing permissible and to minimise the gravity of the commandment. Allah rays :

"Surely We have revealed the reminder and We will most
surely be its guardian". (xv-9).

And He also says :

"Thus (it was) that We might turn away from him evil and
indecency ; surely he was one of Our sincere servants." (xii-24).

Then the protection and guardianship of Allah will be
accompanying you till you meet your Lord by his Mercy. And
it is your portion fixed for you ; and it was withheld from you
during your journey through wildernesses and deserts of desires
and urges of nature, because it would be a heavy burden. So
you were unburdened of it lest it should be heavy on you and
you become weakened and diverted from your purpose and
your objective and this up to the time of your reaching the
threshold of annihilation, and this is the attainment of nearness to Allah and of knowledge of Him and of being particu-

larly favoured with secrets and different kinds of knowledge
and entrance into the sea of lights in such a way that the darkness of nature does not endanger the lights.

So the nature remains in man to the point of the separation
of the soul from the body, in order that the portions may be
fully received, because had the nature disappeared from man he
would have been in the category of the angels and the system
would in that case be distracted and the wisdom of Allah be
frustrated. So the nature will linger in order that you may
take full share of your portions and enjoyments. And this
will be an allowance, not the original things, as the Holy Prophet (peace and blessings of Allah be upon him) has said :

"Three things from your world have been made dear to me—
perfumes and women and the coolness of my eyes is reposed in
prayer".

So when the Holy Prophet (peace and blessings of Allah be
upon him) vanished from the world and what is in it, his portions were returned to him, portions that were withheld from
him while he was on his journey towards his Lord ; so he took
full share of it to be in accord with his Lord and to be pleased
in His act and in obedience to His commandment,—His attributes are holy and His mercy universal and His grace accompanies his saints and Prophets. So the *Wali* is like this in this
matter. His portions and enjoyments are given back to him
after his annihilation and this together with the guarding of the
bounds of law. And this is a return from the destination
towards the start (in the terminology of the *Sufis*).

THE SIXTY-FIRST DISCOURSE

He (may Allah be pleased with him) said :

Every believer is charged with hesitation and scrutiny at the
time of the arrival of portions, in receiving and accepting them
until the commandment of law declares it as permissible and
the Divine knowledge sanctions it as the portion, as the Holy
Prophet (blessings and peace of Allah be upon him) has said :

"Verily the believer scrutinises and the hypocrite pounces
upon (anything that comes to him)."

And he (blessings and peace of Allah be upon him) also
says : "A believer is hesitant" And he (peace and blessings of
Allah be upon him) still further says : "Discard whatsoever
causes doubt in your mind and accept what does not cause such
a doubt."

So a believer hesitates at every kind of articles of food and
drink and dress and affairs of marriage and all other things
which are made accessible to him, so he will not accept any of
these unless a decision is given for him in favour of its permissibility and acceptability by the commandment of law, if one is
in the state of piety ; or unless a decision is given for him in
this regard by the inner commandment if one is in the state of
Wilayat, or unless a decision is given for him in this regard by
the Divine knowledge if one is in the state of *Abdal* and *Ghauth*,
as also by the act of Allah which is the very destiny and this
last state is the state of annihilation.

Then comes another state wherein one receives whatever
comes to one and is made accessible to one provided it is not
taken exception to by the commandment of law or the inner
commandment or the Divine knowledge ; but if these object to
any of these things one refrains from receiving it and discards
it. So this is contrary to the former state wherein hesitation
and delay are predominant whereas in the second the acceptance, reception and the use of the acquired thing is predominant.

Still further comes to him a third state wherein remains just
reception and use of the acquired thing among the blessings
without any interference of any of the three things and this is
the reality of annihilation and in this state the believer becomes
immue from all calamities and infringement of the bounds of
law and all evils are kept away from him as Allah the Exalted
says :

"Thus (it was) that We might turn away from him evil and
indecency ; surely, he was one of Our sincere servants." (xii-
24).

So the servant of Allah becomes protected against all
infringements of the bounds of law and like one who has been
entrusted with His permission with all affairs and who is given

absolute power in all permissible things in order to make easily
accessible to him. So all that comes to him in this position has
been cleared for him of all calamities and distresses and difficulties in this world and in the hereafter, and is in perfect
accord with the purpose of Allah and His pleasure and act,
and there is no state above this and this is the goal. And this
is meant for the chiefs of great *Awliya* who are purified and are
pure, posssessors of secrets—people who have attained the threshold of the state which belongs to Prophets (blessings of Allah
be upon them all).

THE SIXTY-SECOND DISCOURSE

He (may Allah be pleased with him) said :
How strange it is that you should often say that so and so
attained nearness to Allah and so and so has been kept away
and so and so has been favoured with gift and so and so has
been deprived of it and so and so has been enriched and so and
so has been empoverished and so and so has been kept healthy
and so and so has been made ill and so and so has been exalted
and so and so has been rendered low and so and so has been
praised and so and so has been reproached and so and so has
been made truthful and so and so has been belied ! Do you not
know that He is one and that the one loves oneness in the
matter of love and loves one who is singular in his love to Him?
If He draws you near to Himself through something else than
Himself, your love for Him will become faulty thereby and will
be scattered. Because many a time there enters into your mind
an attachment to one through whose hands appears the
attainment of a blessing. As a result, the love of Allah in your
heart suffers deficiency ; and He, the Mighty, the Glorious, is
jealous and does not love an associate: so He restrains the
hands of other people from reaching you for assistance and the
tongues of others from singing your praise and the legs of
others from coming to you so that they may not divert you
from Him. Have you not heard the saying of the Holy Prophet
(peace and blessings of Allah be upon him) ?
Hearts are so constituted that one cannot help loving a

person who has done him a favour and must be repulsed from one who has caused him any harm.

So He withholds in all possible ways people from doing an act of favour to you until you realise His unity and love Him and become His wholly and safely, outwardly and inwardly, in your movements and restful conditions so much so that you do not see any good excepting what comes from him, nor any evil excepting what comes from Him, and you become vanished from the creation and from your own self and from your desires and from your purpose and from your wishes and from all that is besides Allah.

Then the hands are made to open towards you with ampleness, munificence and gifts and the tongues are released with your praise. So you are nourished with lavish care through all times in this world and then in the hereafter.

So do not be ill-mannered: Look at one who looks at you and be attentive to one who is attentive to you and love one who loves you and respond to one who calls you and extend your hand to one who keeps you firm against falling, who brings you out from the darkness of your ignorance and saves you from perishing and washes you clean from your dirts and purifies you from your filth and will release you from your dead and stinking self and from your low desires and from your unredeemed self which commands evil and from your misguided associates who are your devils and from your ignorant friends who are waylayers on the way to Allah and who stand between you and everything that is decent and precious and attractive.

How long will you sick to your animal nature and to the creation and to your desire and to your disobedience and to the world and to the life after death and to whatever is besides Allah ? Why are you so away from the Creator of things and from one who has brought everything to existence, who is the first and last, the manifest and the secret, the returning point and the issuing point of things, and to whom belongs the heart and the solace of the souls, and the unburdening of burdens and the giving of gifts and bestowing of favours ?

THE SIXTY-THIRD DISCOURSE

He (may Allah be pleased with him) said :

I saw in a dream as if I was saying : "Oh you ascribing partnership to your Lord in your mind by your own self and in your outward conduct by His creation and in your actions by year desires!" At this a man who was by my side said: "What is this statement?" So I said : "It is a kind of spiritual knowledge."

THE SIXTY-FOURTH DISCOURSE

He (may Allah be pleased with him) said :

A certain matter had kept my mind very disturbed one day. My inner self was agitated under its burden and was asking for ease and comfort and a way out. I was asked what I wanted. I said : "I wanted death which has no life in it and a life which has no death in it."

So I was asked what kind of death it is that has no life in it and what kind of life it is that has death in it. I said: "The death that has no life in it is my death from my own species so that I do not see them either in benefit or in harm, and my death from my own self and my own desire and my own purpose and my own wishes in my worldly life as well as in my life after death, so much so that I do not live in any of these and am not found in them. And as for the life that has no death in it, it is my life with the act of my Lord in such a manner that I have no existence in it and my death in it is my existence with him. Since I have attained understanding this has been the most precious of all purposes of mine."

THE SIXTY-FIFTH DISCOURSE

He (may Allah be pleased with him) said :

Why are you angry with your Lord on account of delay in the acceptance of your prayers ? You say that you have been forbidden to ask from people and have been commanded to ask from Him and that while you pray to Him, He does not respond to your prayer. My reply to you is : Are you a free man or are you a bondman ? So if you say you are a free man you are an unbeliever. And if you say you are a slave, I should ask you, Are you finding fault with your master on account of delay in the acceptance of your prayer and are entertaining doubt in His wisdom and His mercy with regard to you and the whole of the creation and in His knowledge of all their affairs ? Or are you not finding fault with Him ? So if you do not blame Him and acknowledge His Wisdom and purpose and sense of practical necessity in your case in delaying the acceptance of prayer, it is incumbent on you to be thankful to him because He has adopted the best procedure for you and a thing which is a blessing and which prevents harm. And if you are blaming Him in this matter you are an unbeliever on account of your finding fault with Him because thereby you are ascribing to Him injustice whereas He is not unjust to His servants in fact. He does not admit of any injustice and it is impossible for Him to be unjust, seeing that He is your master, the master of everything ; and the master has the fullest control over his possession to the measure of his liking. So the term "injustice" is not applicable to Him because for sooth an unjust person is he who interferes in the possession of another person without the latter's permission.

So do not give way to resentment against Him in His action manifesting itself through you, even if it goes against your liking and against the desires of your self and even though outwardly it may be injurious to you. So it is incumbent on you that you should adopt thankfulness and patience and concord and pleasure with Him and should renounce resentment and accusation and the attitude of disobedience of your mind and its desires—things that will lead you astray from the path of Allah, and it is also incumbent on you to persist in prayers and in the sincerity of solicitation and in entertaining good notion about your Lord and in waiting for better times and in having faith in His promise and in exhibiting modesty in your attitude towards Him and in showing accord with His commandment and in guarding His unity and in your quickness in carrying out His orders and in keeping away from indulging in things He has prohibited and in assuming the position of a dead man at the time of the manifestation of His decree with regard to you and of His act in respect of you.

And if it is unavoidable that you should blame and be lacking in confidence at all cost, then to blame your own self which by its very nature commands evil and disobedience to its Lord, the Mighty, the Glorious, is better than the other course, and your ascribing injustice to this self of yours is more proper than your ascribing it to your Lord so beware of being in accord with your own self and of being friendly with it and of being pleased with its action and its word in all conditions, because it is the enemy of Allah and your enemy, is a friend of the enemy of Allah and of your enemy, viz. the accursed devil. It is the vicegerent of the devil and its spy and is sincerely devoted to him.

So fear Allah and again fear Allah. Beware, beware. Make good your escape ! make good your escape ! Accuse your own self and ascribe injustice to it and read to it the word of Allah :

"Why should Allah chastise you if you are grateful and believer ?" (iv-147).

Also the following words

"This is because of what your hands have sent before, and surely Allah is not unjust to His servants." (iii-181).

Also remind it of these words of Allah:

"Surely Allah does not do any injustice to people but the people are unjust to their own selves." (x-44).

Read to your self these words and other verses of the Quran to this effect and also the sayings of the Holy Prophet (may Allah's peace and blessings be upon him). Be at war with your own self for the sake of Allah. And be inimical to it on His behalf and fight with it and try to kill it and be a commander of His forces and army, because your self is the greatest enemy amongst the enemies of Allah. Allah has said:

O Dawood, discard your desire because there is no one who disputes with Me in My possession excepting the desire of man."

THE SIXTY-SIXTH DISCOURSE

He (may Allah be pleased with him) said:

Do not say: "I will not pray for anything to Allah because if the prayed-for object has been allotted to me it will surely come to me whether I ask for it or not. Whereas if it is not in my lot, He will not give it to me by my asking for it." No, you should ask from Him all that you want and need of good things of this world and of the hereafter provided there be nothing in it which is forbidden and injurious, because Allah has commanded us to ask from Him and has urged us to that end. He says: "Call on Me; I will accept your prayers" (xl-60).

He also says: "Ask from Allah His favour." (iv-32).

And the Holy Prophet (peace and blessings of Allah be upon him) says : "Ask from Allah while you are fully confi-dent of the acceptance of your prayer." And he (peace and blessings of Allah be upon him) says : "Pray to Allah with the palms of your hands."

And there are other sayings of the Holy Prophet (peace and blessings of Allah be upon him) like this. And do not say : "Surely I have prayed for certain things to Him but He has not given them to me, so now I will not ask anything from him." You should rather persist in your prayer to Him. So if it is a thing which is allotted to you He will send it to you after you have asked for it and this will increase you in faith and certainty and in realising His unity and will help you in keeping away from asking from people and in turning to Him in all your conditions and in your confidence that all your needs are ful-filled by Him.

And if it is not in your lot He will give you self-sufficiency with regard to it and will give you pleasure with Himself, the Mighty, the Glorious, in spite of your poverty. And if you are in the midst of poverty and illness, He will make you pleased with such troubles. And if it is a question of debt He will turn the heart of the lender from an attitude of severe demand into that of gentleness towards you and of deferment and of provision of facility up to the time when it is easy for you to repay the debt or to a mood which will make Him write off the debt or make a reduction in it. Then if it is not written off in your behalf or reduced in this world, Allah, the Mighty, the Glorious, will give you in the life after death a considerable amount of reward in exchange for what He has not given you in response to your prayer in this world because He is generous, free from want and merciful.

So He will not disappoint one who prays to Him in this world and in the hereafter. So it cannot but bring in some benefit and acquisition, sooner or later. A saying of the Holy Prophet (may Allah's peace and blessings be upon him) runs to the effect that the believer will see in the record of his deeds on the Day of Judgment some acts of merit which he had not performed nor was aware of. So he will be asked, "Do you recognise them ?" He will say, "I do not know where these are from." So it will be said to him :

"Surely this is in recompense of your petitions which you made in your worldly life and this is because in making these prayers to Allah, the Mighty, the Glorious, you had been remembering Him and acknowledging His unity and keeping a thing in its proper place and giving a person his due and discarding the ascription of might and power to your own self and renouncing pride and vanity and boastfulness, and all these constitute good deeds, for which there has been a reward in the eye of Allah, the Mighty, the Glorious.

THE SIXTY-SEVENTH DISCOURSE

He (may Allah be pleased with him) said :
Whenever you have fought with your own self and overcome it and killed it by the sword of opposition, Allah will revive it and it will contend with you and ask from you satisfaction of desires and relishing of enjoyments from among sinful things as well as things permissible, with the result that you are to return to a struggle with your own self and attempt to overcome it, so that a reward may be written for you every time afresh. And this is the meaning of the saying of the Holy Prophet (blessings and peace of Allah be upon him) :

"We have returned from a minor *Jihad* (meaning warfare with the unbelievers) to a major *Jihad*".

He meant to say that (the return is) a towards struggle with one's own self in its perpetuity and recurrence—a struggle against desires and enjoyments and against the self being engrossed in sinful things. And this is the meaning of the word of Allah :

"And serve your Lord till the certainty (death) comes to you". (xv-99).

Allah has commanded His Prophet (may peace and blessings of Allah be upon him) to serve Him and this implies opposition to man's own self because all service is declined by the self which desires just the opposite of it till the coming of certainty (death). And if it be asked : how could the self of the Prophet of Allah decline service seeing that he had no fleshly desires ? and that Allah says :

"He does not speak from his own desire : that it is nought but revelation that is revealed". (liii-84).

It will be said to you that He addresses His Prophet (may peace and blessings of Allah be upon him) in these words just to make an affirmation with regard to this subject, so it becomes applicable to the general condition of his followers up to the moment of the advent of the Hour. Then He, the Mighty, the Glorious, gave His Prophet (may peace and blessings of Allah be upon him) power to cover his own self, so that it might not harm him nor oblige him to struggle against his own self and this distinguishes him from his followers. So when a believer persists in a spiritual struggle like this up to the point of the coming of death and meets his Lord with a drawn sword besmeared with the blood of his self and his desires. He gives him what He has guaranteed him of the paradise in His words :

"And as for him who fears to stand before his Lord and forbids the soul from low desires, then surely the garden that is his abode." (lxxix. 41).

So when He has made him enter the garden He will make it his abode and resting place and the place of return which will make him secure from any shifting and transference to any other place or return to the worldly abode ; and will renew for him from day to day and from hour to hour all kinds of provisions for pleasure and will bestow on him all kinds of dress and ornaments which will never end nor be exhausted, as He has been renewing in this world every day, every hour and every moment the struggle against his own self and desires.

But as for the unbeliever and the hypocrite and the sinner when they have left struggle with their own selves and their desires in this world and followed and made alliance with the

devil and became mixed with various kinds of sins of unbelief
and polytheism and such like things till death comes to them
without their having adopted Islam and repented, Allah will
make them enter the fire which is prepared for the unbelievers
as is indicated in His words :

"Then be on your guard against the fire of which men and
the stones are the fuel ; it is prepared for the unbeliever"
(ii-24).

So when He has made them enter it and made it their place
of flight and place of return and place of refuge, it will burn
their skins and their flesh and He will give them fresh skin and
fresh flesh according as He says :

"So often as their skins are thoroughly burned, We will
change them for other skins". (iv-56).

He, the Mighty, the Glorious, will do so with them because
of their having made an alliance with their own selves and
desires in this world in the mátter of committing sins. So the
inmates of fire will have their skin and flesh renewed at all
times so as to cause them chastisement and pain thereby. Whereas the people of the garden will have their provisions of pleas-
sure renewed at all times so as to cause an intensification of the
gratification of their desires and pleasures which are with them.
And this will be as a result of their struggle with their own
selves in order to make them accord (with the will of Allah) in
this world's life, and this is what is meant in the saying of the
Holy Prophet (peace and blessings of Allah be on him) : "This
world is the culture grounds for the hereafter"

THE SIXTY-EIGHTH DISCOURSE

He (may Allah be pleased with him) said :
When Allah grants the prayer of a servant of His and gives
him what he asks for. His own purpose does not thereby
become frustrated, nor that with the writing of which the pen
has become dried (that is the final decree of Providence) and
that which has already occurred to the Divine knowledge. On
the contrary, such a prayer is in conformity with the object of
the Lord and occurs timely. So the acceptance of the prayer
and the fulfilment of the need take place in due time and in

accordance with a set plan which the Destiny has arranged beforehand in the beginning of time and which have been waiting to see fulfilment at the appointed hour. This is what the people of knowledge have said in explaining the Divine word : "Every moment He is in a new state." (lv-29).

This means that Allah drives the allotments of Destiny towards the appointed times. Thus Allah does not give any person anything in this world by merely the prayer proceeding from him and similarly He does not turn away anything from him through mere prayer and it is said that the saying of the Holy Prophet (may Allah's peace and blessings be upon him) to this effect means that the decree of fate is not averted excepting by that prayer with regard to which it is decreed that it will so avert such a decree. And in the same manner no one will enter the paradise in the life hereafter through his good deeds alone but by the mercy of Allah. And yet the servants of Allah will be given ranks in the paradise according to their deeds. And there is a saying of Hazrat Ayisha Siddiqah (may Allah be pleased with her) that she asked the Holy Prophet (peace and blessings of Allah be on him) : "Will anyone enter the paradise just by his deeds ?" The Holy Prophet (peace and blessings of Allah be upon him) replied : "No, but by the mercy of Allah." Then she said, "And not even you ?" So he said, "Yes, not even I, unless Allah covers me by His mercy." And with this he placed his hand on his head.

And he did this to indicate that no one has any right as against Allah nor is He under any obligation to fulfil any promise. He rather does what He wills, chastises whom He wills, forgives whom He wills, and shows mercy to whom He wills, and bestows favour on whom He wills, and He has absolute power to do whatever He likes. He cannot be questioned with regard to what He does, whereas His servants will be questioned, and He gives sustenance to whom He wills by His favour and mercy, and withholds His favours from whomsoever He likes in exercise fof His justice. And it cannot be otherwise, since the creation from the Divine throne down to the very bottom of this earth, which is at the seventh layer downwards of this planet, is in His possession and is His creation. There

is no master for them excepting Him and no creator for them
besides Him and Allah has said : "Is there any creator besides
Allah ?" (xxxv-3). And He has also said : "Is there any Go d
with Allah ?" (xxvii-63) And He has also said : "And do yo u
know anyone who is equal to Him ?" (xix-65).

He also says :

"Say : Oh Allah ! Master of the kingdom ! Thou givest the
Kingdom to whomsoever Thou pleasest and take away the king-
dom from whomsoever Thou pleasest and Thou exaltest whom
Thou pleasest and abasest whomsoever Thou pleasest : in Thine
hand is the good ; surely Thou hast power over all things......
Thou givest sustenance to whom Thou pleasest (xxv-26).

THE SIXTY-NINTH DISCOURSE

He (may Allah be pleased with him) said :

Do not ask from Allah, the Mighty, the Glorious, anything
other than the forgiveness of past sins and protection from sins
in the present and the future and the power of goodly obedience and to perform commandments and to abstain from prohibited things and to be pleased with the bitterness of the
decree of Providence and to be patient in the face of the severi
ties of calamities and to be thankful for the abundance of comforts and gifts and lastly to die with a good end of the life and
be united with the Prophets and *Siddiqs* and *Shahids* and
virtuous men who are a goodly band of companions. And do
not ask from Him things like the removal of poverty and calamity and the advent of affluence and ease, but ask instead
leisure with what He has allotted and provided, and ask from
Him perpetual protection in what He has placed you in the
midst of and landed you in and involved you in, up to the time
that He transfers you from that state to another and to one
that is the opposite of it, because you do not know wherein lies
good—in poverty or affluence, in calamity or in ease. He has
kept the knowledge of things hidden from you and He is alone
in His knowledge of good and evil of things, and there is a
tradition handed down by Hazrat Umar bin al-Khattab (may
Allah be pleased with him) in which he is reported to have
said :

"It matters little to me in what condition I see the morning of the day—whether it brings to me what I dislike or it brings what I love, because I do not know in which of them lies good".

He said so on account of his perfect pleasure with the management of Allah and his satisfaction with His choice and decree. Allah says :

"Fighting is enjoined on you and it is distasteful to you and may be you dislike a thing which is good for you and may be you like a thing which is bad for you." (ii-216).

God knows what is good and what is bad and you do not know it.

And continue in this till your desire vanishes and your self is broken, humbled and overpowered and brought into subjection ; then your purpose vanishes as also your wishes and all existences go out from your heart and nothing remains therein save Allah. Then is your heart filled with the love of Allah and your motive for attaining Him becomes sincere. After this your purpose is returned to you by His command together with your desire to have some enjoyments of this world and of the hereafter and then you will ask these things from Allah and seek them in obedience to His command and as a course of harmony with Him. If He makes a gift to you, you will be thankful for it and will appropriate the same and if He witholds from you anything you will not be annoyed on that account and will experience no change in your mind and will not find fault with Him on that score, because you have not been seeking it from your desire and your purpose since your heart is free from these things and you have not entertained any wish for these things but only followed the commandment of Allah through your petition to Him and peace be on you.

THE SEVENTIETH DISCOURSE

He (may Allah be pleased with him) said:

How can it be a good thing for you to be conceited in the matter of your deeds and to be conscious of the achievements to your self in this regard and to seek returns for them while saying that all these are from the power given by Allah and through His help and strength, purpose and favours? And if it be a case of discarding sin, so this again is through the immunity and protection provided by him and help given by Him. How can you be without thankfulness on that account and without acknowledging all these blessings which He has made available to you? Why is this spirit of disobedience and ignorance that you should feel proud of an act of courage which is not yours and of an act of generosity and liberality of monetary help which belongs to others? When you cannot kill your enemy without the help of some valiant person who strikes your enemy and you only complete the act of killing and without this other man you would have been felled and prostrated yourself instead of your enemy ; nor could you have spent some of your money unless there were some truthful, generous and trustworthy man to stand security on your behalf for an equal amount of money, but for whose assurance and promises inviting your covetousness and standing security on your behalf, you could never have given in charity even a grain from your wealth — if all this is so, how can you be so proud just on account of your own deed ?

The best course for you is to give thanks to and praise the helper and to praise Him continuously and to ascribe your achievement to Him in all conditions of your life unless it be the evil and sins and blames. When it comes to these latter things you should ascribe them to your own self. You should ascribe to your own self injustice and bad manners and blame it for these, for it deserves these things more than anyone else, since it is the seat of all evil and commands everything bad and useless. And if He, the Mighty, the Glorious, is the creator of your deeds and your efforts, you are the maker of efforts and He is the Creator of them. This is what some of the learned in Divine knowledge mean when they say : "The act will come and you cannot escape from it."

There is also a saying of the Holy Prophet (may Allah's peace and blessings be upon him) to this effect :

"Perform good deeds and draw near to Allah, and direct yourself aright, since to everyone is made easy whatever he is created for".

THE SEVENTY-FIRST DISCOURSE

He (may Allah be pleased with him) said :

You must be either the one or the other of the two things. You are either a seeker or the object sought for. If you are a seeker or a disciple you must be burdened and be a carrier of burden carrying everything difficult and heavy. This is because you are a seeker and a seeker is to toil and is reproved until he attains his object and succeeds in obtaining his beloved and attains his goal. And it does not beseem you that you should flee from troubles which befall you in the matter of your life and wealth and the members of your family and children until you are relieved of your burden and the load is taken away from you and your sufferings are removed from you as also your humiliation. So you will be kept secure from all kinds of vices and dirt and filth and humiliation and abasement and illness and sufferings and neediness to people. So you will be made to enter the category of people who are loved by Allah and nourished by Him lavishly and are His objects.

But if you are the thing sought for, then do not blame Allah if He made a calamity befall you in the same way and you should by no means entertain doubt with regard to your position and rank with Him, because He has put you in trial in order to make you attain the status of high personages and He wants to raise your position to the position of *Awliya* and *Abdal*. Do you like that your position be lower than theirs or that your robe of honour and light and blessings be other than what are theirs ; and even if you are pleased with your inferior status, Allah the Mighty, the Glorious, will not be pleased with it. In this connection He says : "And Allah knows and you do not know." (ii-232).

He has chosen for you what is more elevated and brighter and higher and better, whereas you decline to have it.

Then if you say : how is it right that the perfected devotee should be put into trial when according to your division and description the trial is meant for the lover, whereas the favourite one of Allah is the beloved ? We say : We have mentioned the rule first and have spoken of the possible exception next. There are no two opinions that the Holy Prophet (peace and blessings

of Allah be upon him) was the chief among the beloved and at
the same time was one who was tried most. The Holy Prophet
(peace and blessings of Allah be upon him) has said :

"I have been affrighted so much on account of Allah that
no one else is threatened like me and I have been made to
suffer so much on account of Allah that no one else is made to
suffer equally and there have come on me thirty days and nights
on which we had not so much of food as could be hidden under
the armpit of Bilal."

He has further said :

"Surely we prophets are most severely tried ; next to us
come those of lower grade and so on."

Still further he says :

"I am the best in the knowledge of Allah and most afraid
of Him among you all."

Now, how can the beloved be tried and affrighted seeing
that he is the favourite and the perfect devotee ? This is so
only because the object is to make them attain, as we have
already pointed out, the higher stations of heaven, and because
the grades of heavenly life are not raised excepting through
good deeds in the worldly life. The worldly life is a cultivation
ground of the life hereafter and the good deeds of the Prophets
and *Awliya* after the performance of commandments and prohibitions consist in patience and pleasure and reconcilement in
the midst of trial. It is then that the trial is removed from
them and they are made to experience the blessings of Allah
and His favour and lavish care till they meet the Lord in the
eternity.

THE SEVENTY-SECOND DISCOURSE

He (may Allah be pleased with him) said :

Those who got to the markets from among the people of
religion, in observation of the institutions of religion, or in
performance of such commandments of Allah at those concerning
the congregational prayers on Friday or other religious con-
gregations or to fulfil other needs with which they may be con-
fronted, are of several kinds.

Some of them are such that when they go to the market and
see in it various kinds of provisions for the gratification of the
senses and for enjoyments, they are captivated thereby and their
hearts become entangled therein and they thus fall into trial,
and this becomes a cause of their ruin and of discarding their
religion and its institutions and makes them incline towards
yielding to their lower nature and towards following their
passions unless of course Allah looks after them by His mercy
and protecting power and by His providing them with patience
to struggle against these temptations; it is by this means that
they can remain safe.

Then there are others among them who, when they see these
things and are on the point of being ruined, return to their
reasoning sense of religion and exercise selfcontrol with an
effort and drink the bitterness of discarding them. These are
like valiant warriors in the cause of religion who are helped by
Allah to assume control over their own selves and natures and
desires and passions. Allah awards them abundance of reward
in the life after death.

In this connection we have it in some of the traditions handed down by the Holy Prophet (peace and blessings of Allah be
on him):

"Seventy acts of virtue are recorded to the credit of a believer
on his discarding the urge of passion while he is overpowered by
it or when he overpowers it."

In another saying of his we read similarly:

"And some of them there are who obtain these enjoyments
and appropriate them and acquire them by the favour and
blessing of Allah in the shape of affluence of worldly wealth and
give thanks to Allah, the Mighty, the Glorious, on account of
them."

While they are still others who neither see nor are aware of
these enjoyments; they are blind to everything excepting Allah,
the Mighty, the Glorious; so they do not see anything besides
Him and are deaf to everything besides Him, so they do not
hear anything besides Him. They are too engaged to look at
anything excepting the Beloved and their urge for Him. So they
are away from what keeps the world occupied. When you see

such persons entering the market place and ask them what they see in the market, they will say: "We do not see anything." Yes, they do see things but they see them with their physical eyes but not with the eyes of the heart. And they see them only casually, not with the eyes of desire. The sight is of the appearance and not of reality. It is an outward sight, not an inward one. So outwardly he sees what is in the market while in his heart he sees the Lord—sometimes His Glory and at others His Grace.

While there are still others who, when they enter the market place, find that their hearts are filled on account of Allah, the Mighty, the Glorious, with mercy for the people in it. So this pity for the people of the market keeps them too occupied to look at things which belong to these people and which are before them. So such people remain engaged, right from the entrance up to the time of their exit, in prayer and in seeking the protection of Allah and intercession for its people, in an attitude of affection and mercy. So their hearts burn to seek their benefit and to prevent their loss, and their tongues remain engaged in the praise of Allah on account of all that He has given them from His blessings and favours. So such people are called the spiritual guards of the cities and the servants of Allah. And if you like you can call them men possessed of knowledge and *Abdal* and men of piety and knower so the unseen and the seen, His beloved and finished object and His vicegerent on earth appointed over His servants, His ambassadors and executors of good, sweet of expression, guides, rightly-guided people and spiritual instructors. A person of this class is, so to speak, a philosopher's stone and the egg of a magpie. The pleasure of Allah and His blessings be on such a person and on everyone who has set his face towards Allah and who attains the summit of spiritual elevation.

THE SEVENTY-THIRD DISCOURSE

He (may Allah be pleased with him) said:

Sometimes Allah informs His *Walis* about the faults and falsehood of another person and his false claims about his actions and words and thoughts and intentions. So the *Wali* of

Allah is made to feel jealous in respect of his Lord and His
Prophet and His religion. So the inner anger and then also the
outer anger are intensified with the thought. How can comfort
be claimed in face of the existence of diseases, both internal
and external, and how can the faith in the unity of Allah be
claimed in face of polytheistic tendencies which amount to
unbelief and which take a man away from nearness to Allah
and in face of an attitude belonging to the enemy, the devil, the
accursed, and to the hypocrites who are sure to be flung and
hurled into the lowest of hell and are sure to remain for ever?
So the mention of the faults of such a person and his evil actions
and his insolence together with his big claims and his presump-
tion to possess the spiritual state of the *Siddiqs* and his attitude
of competition towards those who have annihilated themselves
in the decree and his thus assuming the role of the finished
object of Allah—is made to come out from the tongue of the
Wali.

This is done sometimes on account of the jealousy for the
glory of Allah, the Mighty, the Glorious, and at others for the
refutation of such a false man and as a sort of admonition for
him; and at still others for the predominance of the act of Allah,
the Mighty, the Glorious, and His purpose and His intensity of
wrath over the false man who gives lie to the truth of the *Wali*.
So the *Wali* accused of backbiting the person concerned and it
is asked, "Is the *Wali* permitted to backbite anyone while he is
forbidden to do it? Can he speak of anyone, absent or present,
things which are not known to the rank and file of people?" The
fact is that such a denunciation on their part falls under the
purview of the word of Allah: "Their sin is greater than their
benefit." (ii-219).

Apparently it (such criticism of the *Wali*) is the denunciation
of a disobedient man but in truth it is rousing the wrath of
Allah and taking exception to His act. The condition of such
an objector is bewilderment; it is his duty to remain silent under
such circumstances and to offer submission and to try to find
out its permissibility in the Law and not to raise objection to
the work of Allah and His *Wali* who makes these biting remarks
on account of the false claims of the pretender. If he assumes

this attitude it may result in the uprooting of the evil in him
and be regarded as his repentance and return from his ignorance
and bewilderment. So it will be a sort of attack on behalf of
the *Wali* and will also benefit the self-conceited man who is on
the verge of ruin, on account of his conceit and disobedience;
and Allah guides whomsoever He likes to the right path.

THE SEVENTY-FOURTH DISCOURSE

He (may Allah be pleased with him) said:
The first thing which a man of intelligence should see is the
condition and composition of his own self and then all the
creations and inventions. Then he should infer from them the
existence of their Creator and Originator. Because the creation
indicates the Creator and strong power is an indication of the
wise actor behind it, because all things are in existence through
Him. And it is this which is reported from Ibn Abbas (may
Allah be pleased with him and his father) in his comment on
the word of Allah:

"And He has made subservient to you all that is in the
h eavens and in the earth."

It is reported from the aforesaid in explanation of this verse
that:

In everything there is an attribute from the attributes of
Allah and every name is a sign for one of His names; so surely
you are between His names and His attributes and works, inwardly through His power and outwardly through His wisdom.
He is manifest in His attributes and concealed in His person.
His person is concealed in His attributes and His attributes are
concealed in His works. And He has revealed His knowledge
through His will and He has expressed His will in movements.
And He has concealed His skill and His workmanship and
expressed His workmanship through His will. So He is hidden
in His invisibility and He is manifest in His wisdom and power.
"There is nothing like a likeness of Him and He is the Hearing
a nd the Seeing." (xlii-11).

Surely many secrets of spiritual knowledge have been brought
to surface by this statement which cannot come to the knowledge
of anyone unless he has a heart which has a lamp of spiritual

knowledge in it. And this privilege of this great man is due to
the fact that the sinless hands of the Holy Prophet (may Allah's
peace and blessings be upon him) were raised in earnest prayer
for him saying: "O Allah! give him understanding of religion
and teach him the interpretation."

May Allah shower on us the same blessings which He
showered on such like people and may He gather us in their
company on the Day of Resurrection together with their
sanctity A'meen.

THE SEVENTY-FIFTH DISCOURSE

He (may Allah be pleased with him) said:

I admonish you to fear Allah and to obey Him and to adopt
the externals of law and purity of heart and self-control and
cheerful appearance and the habit of making gifts of useful
things and removal of suffering and poverty and the guarding of
the sanctity of spiritual people and good dealing with the fellow-
members of society and good counsel for the youngsters and to
discard enmity with companions and to refrain from hoarding
and to discard the companionship of those who do not belong
to the class of spiritual pilgrims and to render help in matters
religious and worldly. And the reality of religious poverty is
that you should not convey your needs to one who is like you
and the reality of affluence is that you should be above the need
of creatures like yourself, *Tasawwuf* (spiritual culture) is obtained
not through discussion and talk but through hunger and giving
up of things liked and approved of. And do not keep your
knowledge in the forefront while approaching a *Darvish*; rather
keep gentleness as the leading demeanour, because a display of
knowledge will make him uncomfortable whereas gentleness will
make him feel at home. And *Tasawwuf* is based on eight
qualities : (1) Generosity like that of Hazrat Ibrahim (Abraham)
(2) Cheerful submission like that of Hazrat Ism'ail (Ishaq-
Issac) (3) Patience like that of Hazrat Yaqub (Jacob) (4) Prayer
like that of Hazrat Zakariyya (Zachariah) (5) Poverty like that
of Hazrat Yahya (John) (6) Wearing of woollen clothes like
that of Hazrat Musa (Moses) (7) Travelling about like that of

Hazrat Isa (Jesus) and (8) a life of poverty with resignation and content like that of Prophet Mohammad (peace and blessings of Allah be upon him and all the rest).

THE SEVENTY-SIXTH DISCOURSE

He (may Allah be pleased with him) said :

I admonish you that you should associate with the rich with dignity and with the poor with humility. And it is incumbent on you to adopt humility and sincerity and this latter quality amounts to perpetual vision of the Creator. And do not blame Allah in respect of worldly means and be humble before Him in all conditions and do not damage the right of your brother relying on the fact that between you and him there is a friendship. And you should keep company with the *darvishes* with humility and good manners and liberality and kill your self till you regain your life in spirituality. And the people who are nearest to Allah, the Mighty, the Glorious, are those who are most large-hearted in their behaviour. And the best of deeds is to guard one's own self from being inclined to what is besides Allah, the Great. And you should keep on exhorting people to stick to truth and patience. And it is enough for you to keep company with the *darvishes* and to serve the *Awliya*.

And a *darvish* is he who is indifferent to everything besides Allah. And to attack one who is beneath you is cowardice and to do the same thing with one who is above you is shamelessness; whereas to attack one who is equal to you is bad manners. To adopt the life of a *darvish* and of a *sufi* needs an effort ; and do not mix it up with anything which is in the nature of a joke. May Allah give us strength and you too. O *Wali* ! it devolves on you to keep on remembering Allah in all conditions because it brings together all the good things and it is also your duty to adhere to the covenant of Allah because it wards off all injurious things. And it is also a duty of yours to remain prepared to meet all the events decreed by Allah, because they are bound to happen.

And know that you will be asked about your movements and your restful conditions; so keep yourself engaged with what is most suitable for a particular time and save your organs from useles occupations. It is further your duty to obey Allah and His Prophet and those who rule in the latter's place. Give them their dues and do not ask from them what is due from them and pray too for them in all conditions. It is also necessary that you should think well of Muslims and bear good intentions in respect of them and try to secure for them everything that is good and that you should not spend any night while entertaining anything evil for any of them in your heart, nor any grudge nor any enmity.

It is also necessary that you should pray for him who has been unjust to you and should fear Allah, the Mighty the Glorious. And it is also your duty to eat the lawful things only and to inquire from people possessed of the knowledge of Allah in matters which you do not know. You should also cultivate modesty in respect of Allah, the Mighty, the Glorious, and keep company with Allah and keep company with what is besides Allah only to the extent of your requirements of the companionship of Allah.

And give in charity from your wealth every morning, and in the night offer the funeral prayer for everyone who has died among the Muslims on that day. And when you have finished your *Maghrib* (early evening) prayer, invoke a prayer of *istikhara* (seeking good in one's affairs). And you should repeat morning and evening seven times: *Allahumma ajirna minan nar*, meaning: "O Allah! protect us from fire." And stick to the prayers: *Auzu-billah-is-smai-il-Alim minash Shaitan-ir-Rajim*, meaning: "I seek the refuge of Allah, the Hearing, the Knowing from Satan the accursed."

And then proceed to the glorification of Allah with the concluding words of Sura "Hashr," (lix-22-24) viz.

"He is Allah besides Whom there is no God: Knower of the unseen and the seen; He is the Beneficent, the Merciful; besides Whom there in no God; the King, the Holy, the Author of peace, the Granter of security: Guardian over all, the Mighty, the Supreme, the Possessor of every greatness. Glory be to Allah, from what they set up (with Him).

He is Allah, the Creator, the Maker, the Fashioner. His are the most excellent names ; Whatever is in the heavens and the earth declares His glory ; and He is the Mighty, the Wise.

Allah alone is the giver of strength and the helper, because there is no might and power excepting in Allah, the High, the Great.

THE SEVENTY-SEVENTH DISCOURSE

He (may Allah be pleased with him) said :

Be with Allah, the Mighty, the Glorious, as if no creation exists. And be with the creation as if there is no self in you. And when you are with Allah, the Mighty, the Glorious, without the creation you will get Him and vanish from every other thing, and when you are with the creation without your self you will do justice and help the path of virtue and remain safe from the hardships of life. And leave everything outside the door while you are entering in your solitude and enter therein alone. And when you have done so, you will see your friend in your solitude with your inner eye and will experience what is besides the creation and then your self will vanish and in its place will come the command of Allah and His nearness. And at this point your ignorance will be your knowledge and your distance will be your nearness and your silence will be your remembrance of Allah and your bewilderment will prove friendship. O you man ! there will be nothing left there at this stage excepting the Creator and the created. So if you have adopted the Creator, then say to the rest :

"Surely they are my enemies but the Lord of the worlds is my friend". (xxvi-77).

Whoever has tasted it, has come to know it.

He was asked: "How can one in whom the bitterness of bile predominates taste sweetness ?" In reply he said, "He should with an effort keep away the sensual desires from himself. O you man ! when a believer does a good deed his animal self changes into his heart (i.e. in response to the dictates of the heart). And the self attains the consciousness of the heart ; then this heart changes into a secret ; then the secret undergoes another change and becomes annihilated ; then the annihilation passes through another transformation and becomes another existence." He further observed : The friends have an access through every door. O you man ! the annihilation (self-effacement) is to deny all creations and transform your nature into

the nature of the angels ; then vanishing from the nature of
the angels and then getting back to the first way ; and then
your Lord will water you as much as He likes and cultivate
you as much as He likes. If you want this stage you should
adopt Islam and then submission to the decree of Allah, and
then acquire the knowledge of Allah and then realise Him and
then exist in Him, and then you get such an existence you will
wholly belong to Him. Piety is a work of an hour and
abstemiousness of two hours and knowledge of Allah is a work
for all times.

THE SEVENTY-EIGHTH DISCOURSE

He (may Allah be pleased with him) said :

There should be ten characteristics of those who are engaged in spiritual struggles and in self-inspection and are deter-
mined to attain the spiritual goal to which they must stick.
And when by the permission of Allah they have established
themselves in these and have made themselves firm, they have
attained to high position.

The first characteristic is that the servant should not swear
by Him whether truthfully or falsely, intentionally or by mistake, because when he consolidates this practice in himself and
makes his tongue habituated to it, this practice will raise him
to a position where he will be able to give up swearing either
intentionally or by mistake. So when he becomes practised in
this, Allah will open for him a door of His lights. He will
recognise the benefit of this in his heart and will find exaltation
in his rank and strength in his determination and patience and
will find praise in the midst of his brethren and dignity in the
midst of his neighbours, so much so that whoever will recognise
him will pay him respect and whoever will see him will be
afraid of him.

The second characteristic is that he should avoid (speaking
of) untruth seriously or out of joke, because if he practises this
and makes it firm in his own self and makes his tongue habituated to it, Allah will open with it His heart and will clarify
his knowledge with it in a manner that it will appear as if he
doesn't know falsehood and when he hears it from others he

will regard it as a great blemish and will be ashamed of it in his own self, and if he prays to Allah to remove it there will be a reward for him.

The third characteristic is that he should beware that when he promises anything to anyone he should not break his promise or he should not make any promise at all. For, surely this will be a (source of) great strength for his affair and a very balanced course for him to follow, since breach of promise belongs to the category of falsehood. So if he does so the door of munificence will be opened to him and the rank of modesty will be allotted to him and love for him will be cast into the minds of men of truth and he will be raised in the sight of Allah.

The fourth is that he should refrain from cursing anything in the creation nor should he cause any harm to anything, not even to an atom or anything less than that, because this quality is among the virtues of the good and the truthful, and acting on this principle a person gets a good end of life under protection of Allah in this life to gether with what Allah has kept reserved for him in the form of his spiritual ranks and He saves him from falling into destruction and protects him from the harm of people and bestows on him mercy for the servants of Allah and nearness to Himself.

The fifth is that he should refrain from praying for any harm to anyone among people, even if he has been treated unjustly. So he should not retaliate either by tongue or by action but bear it patiently for Allah and should not take revenge either by word or by action. So surely this trait raises its possessor to high ranks. When a person gets trained in this he attains a noble position in this world and in the hereafter and love and affection in the hearts of all people who accept the truth, borh near and distant, together with the acceptance of prayer and exaltation in goodness and honour in this world and in the hearts of believers.

The sixth characteristic is that he should not affirm his evidence on polytheism and unbelief and hypocricy of one of those who follow the same *Qiblah* (turning point in prayer). And this trait constitutes the perfection in the following of *Sunnah* (practice of the Holy P rophet (may Allah's peace and blessings be upon him) and is very, very far from any meddling in the knowledge of Allah and also from His chastisement and very close to His pleasure and mercy. Thus it is an honourable and glorious door to Allah the Exalted, who grants it to His believing servant as a reward for his mercy to all people.

The seventh characteristic is that he should refrain from looking at anything of a sinful nature both outwardly and inwardly and should restrain his organs of the body from it because this is an action that is the quickest in bringing reward to the heart and the organs in the immediate worldly life together with what Allah has kept in store and the good things in the hereafter. We pray to Allah that He may do all of us the favour of granting the power to act on these traits and take away the worldly desires from our hearts.

The eighth characteristic is that one should avoid putting any burden on anyone whether it be small or big. On the contrary, he should lift the burden from all people whether on asking or without any asking. So surely this constitutes the highest of honour for the servants of Allah and the cause of nobility for the men of piety and this also provides strength to a man to admonish people to do good or forbid them to do evil. And this constitutes the whole honour and dignity of Allah's servants and of pious men and enables them to enjoin good and forbid evil, and at this stage the whole creation appears to them as of the same position. So when a man is in this stage Allah transforms his heart into a state of needlessness and certainty and reliance on Allah, and Allah does not raise anyone while he is tied up with his worldly desires. The whole creation to such a man possesses equal rights and it should be firmly believed that this is a door of honour for the believers and of dignity for the righteous and it is a door very close to sincerity.

The ninth characteristic is that he should be free from all expectations from men, nor should he feel tempted in his heart by what is with them. So, surely it is a great honour and pure needlessness and great kingdom and glorious pride and clear certainty and clear and healthy reliance on Allah and this is a door from among the doors of reliance on Allah and one of abstemiousness and one which enables one to attain fear of

Allah and imparts perfection to one's religious practices and it further constitutes a sign of complete and exclusive attachment of Allah.

The tenth characteristic is humility, because it is with this trait that the station of the servant is raised high and his position made lofty andy his honour and eminence made perfect in the sight of Allah (glory be to Him) as also in the sight of people, and he is given power over what he desires from among the affairs of the world and of the hereafter. And this is a trait which forms the whole root and branch and the perfection of obedience and with its help the servant of Allah is made to attain the position of the righteous people who are pleased with Allah in ease as well as in difficulties and it is the perfection of piety.

And humility consists in that the servant of Allah does not see anyone from among the people but sees in him superiority over himself and he says: "Perhaps this person is better than myself in the sight of Allah and higher in position." So if he is a small person the servant of Allah says: "This man has not offended Allah and I have offended Him; so undoubtedly he is better than myself." And if the person concerned be a great man, he will say: "This man has served Allah before I have done so." And if the person he sees be a learned man he will say: "This man has been given what has not reached me and he has obtained what I have not, and he knows what I am ignorant of and he acts with knowledge." And if the person concerned be an ignorant man he will say: "This man offended Allah in his ignorance and I have offended Him in spite of my knowledge and I do not know what sort of end I shall meet and what kind of end he will meet." And if this person be an unbeliever he will say: "I do not know; it may be that he will become a Muslim and will end his life with good deed and possibly I will become an unbeliever and will end my life with evil deed."

And this is the door of affection and fear and is a thing of which the accompaniment should be preferred and the final thing which will abide with the servants of Allah.

Thus, when the servant of Allah has become like this, Allah will keep him safe from all calamities and will make him attain the position of the companionship of Allah, the Mighty, the

Glorious, and he becomes among the chosen ones and friends of
Allah and he becomes an enemy of *Iblis* who is the enemy of
Allah. And this state constitutes the gate of mercy with the
attainment of which the door cf pride becomes closed and the
rope of self-conceit is cut as under and the sense of superiority
in his own self in matters religious and worldly and spiritual
becomes discarded, and this is the very essence of servitude and
the cause of abstemiousness and is a sign of devotion to Allah:
so there is nothing better than this. With the attainment of this
state his tongue should cease mentioning the people of the world
and what is vain and no work of his will attain completion
without this step; and malice and conceit and trespassing of
limits will be expelled from his heart in all his conditions, and
his tongue (i.e. talk) will be one and the same in secret as well
as in open; and his purpose will be one in secret as well as in
open; and so will be his words; and the people will be one in his
sight in regard to admonition. And he will not admonish by
mentioning anyone from among the people with an evil reference
or bring any of his actions as an illustration nor will he like
that anyone should be mentioned with a bad reference to him
nor will it please his heart to hear such a reference because this
weakness constitutes a calamity for the servants of Allah and
hardship for the devotees and will lead to the ruin of the ascetic
excepting such of them as are helped by Allah with His mercy
to keep their tongue and heart secure.

THE SEVENTY-NINTH DISCOURSE

Further he (Allah be pleased with him) said:
When the saint was suffering from the illness of which he
died, his son Shaikh Abdul Wahhab said to him: "Give me a
parting admonition which I should act upon after you have left
this world." He said to him: It is incumbent on you to fear
Allah and not fear anyone excepting Him and not to hope from
anyone excepting Him and entrust all your needs to Him. And
do not rely on anyone excepting Him and ask everything from
Him and do not place confidence on anyone besides Him.
Stand by His Unity, stand by His Unity, all are agreed on this.

He further said : When the heart becomes right with Allah,
nothing is felt missing and nothing comes out of the man.

Still further he said : I am the core without the shell.

Still further he said : Others have come to me ; so make
room for them and show courtesy to them. Here there is a
great benefit. And do not make the place congested for these.

He was also heard saying : Upon you be peace, the mercy
of Allah and His blessings. May He protect me and you and
turn with mercy to me and to you. I begin with the name of
Allah unceasingly.

He kept on saying this one day and one night and said :
Woe unto you, I do not fear anything, nor any angel nor even
the angel of death. O angel of death ! it is not you but one who
has befriended me that has been bounteous to me.

Then he gave out a loud cry and this took place on the
evening on which he expired and I am told by his sons Abdul
Razzaq and Musa that he had been raising his hands and
stretching them out and was heard saying : And on you be
peace and the mercy of Allah and His blessings. Repent and
join the line. Presently I will be coming to you.

And he was saying : "Wait". Then came to him the last
moment and the pang of departure from the worldly existence.

THE EIGHTIETH DISCOURSE

He (may Allah be pleased with him) said :

Between myself and you and the creation there is only He
as between the heaven and the earth. So do not guess me by
anyone of them and do not guess anyone of them by me.

Then his son Abdul Aziz asked him about his pain and
about his condition. So he said : Let not anyone ask me about
anything. I am being turned over and over again in the
knowledge of Allah.

It is further reported that his son Abdul Aziz asked him
about his disease. On this he said : Surely no one, neither any
man nor any Jinn, nor any angel knows and understands my
disease. The knowledge of Allah is not diminished by the
command of Allah. The command changes but the knowledge
does not change. The command may be abrogated but not

knowledge. Allah causes to pass away and establishes what
He pleases, and with Him is the basis of the Book.

"And He is not questioned about what He does and it is
they who are questioned." (xxi-23).

The attributes will move on as it is narrated.

And his son Abdul Jabbar asked him : "What part of your
body is ailing ? He said : All the parts of my body are ailing
excepting my heart which has no pain in it and it is sound with
Allah.

Then came to him last moment. He was saying : I seek the
help of Allah with the formula : There is no object of worship
excepting Allah, glory be to Him and be He exalted, the Ever-
living, Who does not fear annihilation ; glory be to Him Who
has established His superiority through His power and overpowered His servants by means of death. There is no object
of worship excepting Allah and Muhammad is the Prophet of
Allah.

I have been told by his son Musa that he was uttering the
word *Taazzaza* and his tongue was unable to utter in correctly,
so he went on repeating it till he uttered this word *Taazzaza*
and prolonged the sound and stressed it so that he uttered it
correctly at last. Then he said : "Allah, Allah, Allah," then
his voice became low and his tongue stuck to his palate and
then his honoured soul left his body—the pleasure of Allah be
upon him. May He allow His blessings to benefit us and
grant us and all the Muslims a good end without abasing us
and putting us in trial and may He thus enable us to join the
men of piety.—*Ameen ! Ameen ! Ameen !*